Disney SQUA

S0-AWK-778

KINGDOM HEARTS
CHAIN OF MEMORIES
OFFICIAL STRATEGY GUIDE

By Elizabeth Hollinger
with Special Contributions by Greg Sepelak

TABLE OF CONTENTS

WELCOME TO CASTLE OBLIVION...

Kingdom Hearts: Chain of Memories is a direct sequel to Kingdom Hearts for the PlayStation 2. It literally picks up right where the ending of the original game left off. Although it's not a requirement to have played the original Kingdom Hearts, it certainly helps to know the storyline.

A TALE CALLED KINGDOM HEARTS

The original Kingdom Hearts told the story of a young boy named Sora and his quest to help his friends and save his world from the corrupting influence of evil creatures known as Heartless.

The story begins in a place called Destiny Islands, where Sora lives with his two best friends, Riku and Kairi. The night before the trio plans to set sail from the islands to explore new worlds, the sky grows dark and dark creatures emerge from the ground. When Riku and Sora go to check on their raft, Riku is swallowed by the darkness, Kairi falls ill, and Sora is presented with an unusual weapon called the Keyblade to fight off the Heartless swarming the area. When the battle ends, Sora encounters a strange door that leads to parts unknown. Thus begins Sora's quest to find his two friends.

In the first town that Sora visits, Traverse Town, three adventurers join Sora on his adventures: Donald Duck, Goofy, and Jiminy Cricket, all retainers of king Mickey. Donald, Goofy, and Jiminy are in search of the Keyblade master under order of their missing king. The four travel to a variety of different worlds, defeating Heartless, making new friends, and sealing keyholes.

" AHEAD LIES SOMETHING YOU NEED— BUT TO CLAIM IT, YOU MUST LOSE SOMETHING DEAR "

Once Sora and his pals seal all of the worlds, Sora finds himself facing his best friend, Riku. It appears that Riku was seduced over to the side of darkness by the sorceress Maleficent and is possessed by a strange scholar named Ansem. Sora soon learns that Riku has been searching for Kairi's lost heart in order to revive her, but the two are fated to fight nonetheless. After defeating Riku, Sora travels to the End of the World and battles Ansem. The story ends with Riku trapped with King Mickey, Kairi alone on Destiny Islands, and Sora, along with Donald, Goofy and Jiminy Cricket, separated from both friends.

Kingdom Hearts: Chain of Memories begins where the original game ends, with Sora and pals in a large field chasing after Pluto, King Mickey's faithful dog. Eventually, the group comes to a crossroads where Sora is told "Ahead lies something you need—but to claim it, you must lose something dear." The roads coalesce into one leading to a shadowy castle known as Castle Oblivion. Perhaps it is here that Sora and his friends will be reunited. And yet, at what cost?

WELCOME TO CASTLE OBLIVION

CHARACTERS

GAME BASICS

CASTLE OBLIVION

SECRETS OF THE GAME

THE CARDS

BESTIARY

THE MAIN CHARACTERS

SORA

Sora is a cheerful boy known for his pure heart and loyalty to his friends. Since the night when Destiny Islands was overrun with Heartless, Sora has traveled far and wide, mastering the Keyblade and protecting the world from the Heartless. In Castle Oblivion, he faces new challenges and new dangers. Fortunately, he is accompanied on this new quest by his stalwart allies Donald Duck, Goofy, and Jiminy Cricket.

WELCOME TO
CASTLE OBLIVION

CHARACTERS

GAME BASICS

CASTLE OBLIVION

SECRETS OF
THE GAME

THE CARDS

BESTIARY

DONALD DUCK

Donald Duck is a Royal Wizard in King Mickey's court. In the original *Kingdom Hearts*, he found a letter from the king explaining his absence. Donald, along with Goofy, decided to leave the castle in hopes of joining the king and helping him defeat the Heartless. Although allied with Sora, they continue with their search to this day. After all, King Mickey might be with Sora's friend Riku.

Donald Duck, as befits the Royal Wizard, is skilled in a variety of magic types. When he is summoned in battle, he casts Cure, Fire, Blizzard, and/or Thunder. The strength of his spells depends upon the combination of cards you use. Stock two or three Donald cards to have him cast the highest levels of those spells.

GOOFY

Goofy is Captain of the Royal Knights of King Mickey's court. Although he is a knight, Goofy tries to avoid fighting whenever possible and instead elects to find non-violent solutions. Still, his loyalty to the king is unquestioned and he will do whatever is required to find and aid his king.

When he is summoned in battle, Goofy races across the battlefield and slams into enemies with his shield. The number of passes he makes depends upon the number of Goofy cards played.

JIMINY CRICKET

In the original *Kingdom Hearts*, Jiminy Cricket was sent by Queen Minnie to accompany Goofy and Donald on their quest to locate the Keyblade Master and King Mickey. Jiminy was responsible for keeping a journal of those events and he plays the same role in this game. Jiminy is the keeper of the Journal, which holds information about all of the characters, Heartless, and cards the group encounters on their quest.

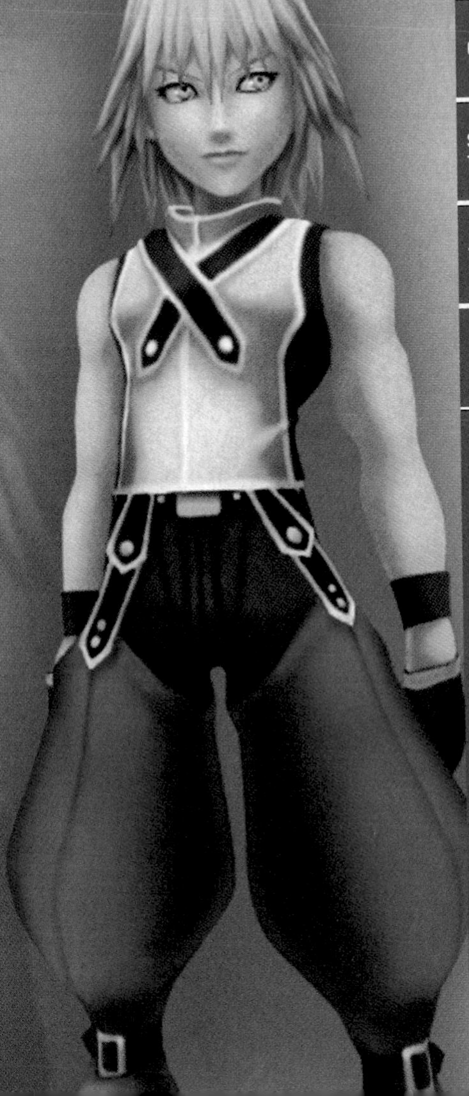

WELCOME TO CASTLE OBLIVION

CHARACTERS

GAME BASICS

CASTLE OBLIVION

SECRETS OF THE GAME

THE CARDS

BESTIARY

RIKU

Riku, Sora, and Kairi grew up as friends on Destiny Islands. Although separated by fate, their friendship remains true, even though Riku's heart has been tainted by darkness. Sora comes to Castle Oblivion in the hopes of finding his friend, knowing little of the adventure that also awaits Riku there...

GAME BASICS

All of the action of *Kingdom Hearts: Chain of Memories* takes place in a large castle called Castle Oblivion. Home to the mysterious Organization, this place has a unique ability to mess with visitors' memories, erasing them and—at times—replacing them with others. The truth behind the castle's powers may never be fully known, but it is up to you to make the journey to the top floor and try to find out.

THE FLOW OF THE GAME

In many respects, this game plays like a recap of the original *Kingdom Hearts* for the PlayStation 2. On each floor of Castle Oblivion, Sora recreates one of the worlds he visited in the original game, from the scenery to the main characters and bosses. Even the monsters have a familiar feel. The Organization is trying to figure out Sora, and probing Sora's memories (and his reactions to them!) seems like a reasonable way to do it.

In each world, Sora must traverse a maze of rooms to reach three story rooms. Inside each story room, a piece of that world's story is revealed. For example, in Traverse Town, the first world, Sora meets his old friend Leon in the first story room to learn a little bit more about the basics of the game's battle system. In the next story room, Sora meets Aerith in her house for more game information. The final story room contains the world's boss, the Guard Armor. Once Sora visits all three story rooms and defeats the boss, the exit to the hallway and the next floor opens up.

After you proceed through the first floor, which recreates the world of Traverse Town, you receive your first set of world cards. At the entrance to each floor, you are asked to choose one of the world cards in your inventory and that world is then recreated in the rooms on the floor. When you run out of world cards, expect to encounter a member of the Organization in the hallway leading to the next floor to win your next batch. Yes, that's *win*, as in you must prove yourself in another boss-type battle.

The structure of events in each world is roughly identical to that described previously. Some worlds have a sub-boss or other type of battle in addition to the main world boss, while others stick to the one boss, one world formula. As you complete each world, you can purchase more cards to fill your battle deck and learn more sleights. By the time you reach the top floors of the castle, you'll be more than ready to take on whatever awaits you!

BASIC CONTROLS

The button commands are pretty basic and easy to learn. Commands are divided into three categories based on whether or not they are used in the Field, on a Menu Screen, or in Battle.

FIELD CONTROLS

These controls are used whenever you are exploring rooms, walking through the hallways connecting the floors, and so on.

Control Pad: Moves Sora around.

A Button: Swing the Keyblade (used to trigger Treasure Spots and initiate Room Synthesis when striking a door); talk to characters with "?" icons over their heads; advance messages (while in conversation).

B Button: Jump; cancel out of Map or Menu screens.

L Button/R Button: Not used in the Field.

START: Brings up the Menu Screen.

SELECT: Displays the World Map of the current floor. This function does not work when Sora is in one of the hallways.

SPECIAL MOVES

When jumping and pressing the Control Pad in the direction of a wall, Sora can grab onto the edge of that wall. When you press Up on the Control Pad, Sora pulls himself up onto the platform. When you press Down on the Control Pad, Sora releases and drops to the ground. This only works with walls/platforms no more than twice Sora's height.

Pulling Sora up to the next level is a great shortcut when the trampolines are out of your way.

BATTLE CONTROLS

These commands are used whenever you are in battle.

Control Pad: Move Sora around the battlefield. Press Left or Right to direct attacks (Sora cannot attack upward or downward). To escape from a battle, run to the left or right side of the screen and press Left or Right button on the Control Pad until the Escape meter fills up and Sora escapes.

A Button: Play a card; hold down to reload cards (while on reload card).

B Button: Jump.

L Button: Cycle through the Card Reel counterclockwise. When you hold down the L Button, the Card Reel quickly spins counterclockwise.

R Button: Cycle through the Card Reel clockwise. When you hold down the R Button, the Card Reel quickly spins clockwise.

L and R Buttons (simultaneously): Stock cards/activate a sleight. (Two-card sleights are activated by pressing the L and R Buttons at the reload card.)

START: Pause battle.

SELECT: Switch between battle Card Reels (normal battle cards and enemy cards).

SPECIAL MOVES

When you tap Left or Right twice on the Control Pad, Sora performs a Dodge Roll. This enables him to slide (or rather, roll) right past enemies, dodging their attacks.

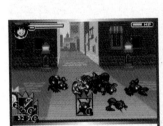

Dodge Rolls are especially helpful when fighting Large Bodies, Defenders, and other large enemies that are difficult to run around.

MENU SCREEN CONTROLS

These commands are used when you are on any of the game's Menu Screens.

Control Pad: Move cursor.

A Button: Confirm commands/selections.

B Button: Cancel commands/selections.

L Button: When used in the Journal, this enables you to cycle backward through the entries.

R Button: When used in the Journal, this enables you to cycle forward through the entries.

START: Return to the Field.

SELECT: Not used.

WELCOME TO CASTLE OBLIVION

CHARACTERS

GAME BASICS

CASTLE OBLIVION

SECRETS OF THE GAME

THE CARDS

BESTIARY

Now that you know how the game works on a basic level, it's time to explore it a little more closely.

ROOM SYNTHESIS

Each floor is comprised of two types of rooms: regular rooms and special rooms. To clear a world, you must get through the regular rooms to the special story rooms. When you open the door to a regular room, you create the room's contents by selecting and playing a map card. There are 22 map cards that govern the way regular rooms look and how many Heartless you encounter inside. Map cards affect other variables inside regular rooms, but that is discussed later.

Hitting a doorway, whether it's open or shut, brings up the Room Creation screen.

The Room Synthesis screen displays the card requirements needed to open that door. For regular rooms, the door requirements are limited to any type of map card of a specific denomination or higher. For example if the door requirement is for a map card with a value of 4, you can use any card marked four or higher to open the door.

The door requirements for regular rooms are set by the number of the card that you used to open the previous room. The doors leading from the entrance room have a requirement of a 1 card or higher. If you use a 1 card to open the first door, then the doors in the next room will require a 2 card or higher. If you don't have a 1 card and choose to use a 5 card, then the door requirements in the next room require a 6 card or higher. To reset the count to 1, simply use a zero card to open the next door.

Each floor also contains up to four special rooms that require the use of a special Keycard, in addition to other map cards, to open. Three of these rooms are story rooms, which are where the storyline behind each world is played out in cut-scenes and where you'll fight that world's boss battle(s). Be prepared for anything when you open the doors to those rooms!

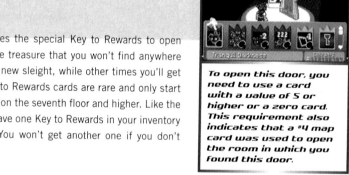

To open this door, you need to use a card with a value of 5 or higher or a zero card. This requirement also indicates that a #4 map card was used to open the room in which you found this door.

Special story rooms appear in yellow on the World Map.

The other special room requires the special Key to Rewards to open and these rooms contain a rare treasure that you won't find anywhere else. Sometimes you'll learn a new sleight, while other times you'll get a new type of battle card. Key to Rewards cards are rare and only start appearing at the end of battles on the seventh floor and higher. Like the other Keycards, you can only have one Key to Rewards in your inventory at a time, so don't hoard it! You won't get another one if you don't use it!

Key to Rewards rooms look like regular rooms on the world map. However, to open them you need the special Key to Rewards card.

The door requirements for special rooms are very specific and set for each floor, regardless of what world you open on that floor and regardless of what number card you used to open the preceding room. Special room door requirements tend to require map cards of a specific color and number in addition to the special Keycard.

The first white card marked with "S" means that you can use any card marked S or higher. The second white card marked with "S" indicates that you can use any card marked S or lower. The blue card indicates that you can use any blue map card of any denomination. Finally the Key of Beginnings card is the final card needed to open the door. Some doors require the use of a card with an exact number; these are marked by an "=" sign after the number. Unlike the door requirements for regular rooms, you cannot use a zero card to override a requirement for a Special room.

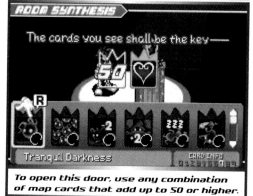

To open this door, use any combination of map cards that add up to 50 or higher.

Map cards fall into four color-coded categories depending on the type of room they create. Red map cards change the number, strength and voracity of the Heartless you encounter in the room. Green map cards change battle conditions, strengthening and/or weakening different types of battle cards or simply adding conditions to battles that you start yourself. Blue map cards create rooms that have a little extra something, like a treasure chest containing a rare item, a sleight, or a Moogle Shop or save point.

Like battle cards, each map card has a number on it ranging from 0-9. These are used in fulfilling door requirements as discussed previously. Map cards are presented at the end of every battle unless you've maxed out your inventory of map cards (you are only allowed to carry 99 map cards at any one time) or you receive an enemy card instead.

The following table illustrates which map cards are available in each World and the probability that you will receive a specific card. This table also lists the card's priority rating from A (high) to C (low). Cards with a higher priority rating are more likely to appear at the end of a battle than those with a lower rating regardless of their probability percentage.

MAP CARD FREQUENCY PER WORLD

Card Name	Traverse Town	Agrabah	Olympus Coliseum	Wonderland	Monstro	Halloween Town
Tranquil Darkness	B 100%	B 80%	B 80%	B 80%	B 80%	B 80%
Teeming Darkness	B 100%	B 80%	B 80%	B 80%	B 80%	B 80%
Feeble Darkness	B 100%	B 80%	B 80%	B 80%	B 80%	B 80%
Almighty Darkness						
Sleeping Darkness	B 100%	B 80%	B 80%	B 80%	B 80%	B 80%
Looming Darkness						
Premium Room		C 100%	C 100%	C 100%	C 100%	C 100%
White Room		C 100%	C 100%	C 100%	C 100%	C 100%
Black Room		C 100%	C 100%	C 100%	C 100%	C 100%
Martial Waking		C 100%	A 20%	C 100%	C 100%	C 100%
Sorcerous Waking		A 20%	B 80%	C 100%	C 100%	C 100%
Alchemic Waking		C 100%	C 100%	C 100%	A 20%	C 100%
Meeting Ground	B 30%	C 100%	C 100%	C 100%	C 100%	B 80%
Stagnant Space		B 80%	B 80%	B 80%	B 80%	B 80%
Strong Initiative		C 100%	C 100%	A 20%	B 80%	A 20%
Lasting Daze		C 100%	C 100%	C 100%	B 80%	B 80%
Calm Bounty		B 80%	B 80%	B 80%	B 80%	
Guarded Trove						
False Bounty						
Moment's Reprieve		B 80%	B 80%	B 80%	B 80%	B 80%
Moogle Room		B 80%	B 80%	B 80%	B 80%	B 80%
Mingling Worlds						
Key to Rewards	0%	0%	0%	0%	0%	0%

Card Name	Atlantica	Never Land	Hollow Bastion	Twilight Town	Destiny Islands	Castle Oblivion
Tranquil Darkness				B 80%		B 70%
Teeming Darkness				B 80%		B 70%
Feeble Darkness				B 80%		B 70%
Almighty Darkness	B 80%	B 80%	B 80%		B 80%	B 70%
Sleeping Darkness				B 80%		B 70%
Looming Darkness	B 80%	B 80%	B 80%		B 80%	B 70%
Premium Room	C 100%	A 20%	C 100%		C 100%	
White Room	A 20%	C 100%	C 100%		C 100%	
Black Room	C 100%	C 100%	A 20%		C 100%	
Martial Waking	C 100%	C 100%	C 100%	C 100%		
Sorcerous Waking	C 100%	C 100%	C 100%	C 100%		
Alchemic Waking	C 100%	C 100%	C 100%	C 100%		
Meeting Ground	C 100%	C 100%	C 100%	B 80%		
Stagnant Space						
Strong Initiative	C 100%	C 100%	C 100%	C 100%		
Lasting Daze	C 100%	C 100%	C 100%	B 80%		B 70%
Calm Bounty						
Guarded Trove	B 80%	B 80%	B 80%		B 80%	B 70%
False Bounty	B 80%	B 80%	B 80%		B 80%	B 70%
Moment's Reprieve	C 100%	C 100%	C 100%	C 100%	C 100%	C 100%
Moogle Room	C 100%	C 100%	C 100%	C 100%	C 100%	C 100%
Mingling Worlds				A 20%	A 30%	
Key to Rewards	10%	10%	10%	20%	30%	40%

WELCOME TO CASTLE OBLIVION

CHARACTERS

GAME BASICS

CASTLE OBLIVION

SECRETS OF THE GAME

THE CARDS

BESTIARY

MAXIMUM NUMBER OF CARDS ATTAINABLE IN THE SAME ROOM

Card Name	Max #	Card Name	Max #
Tranquil Darkness	2	Alchemic Waking	3
Teeming Darkness	4	Meeting Ground	3
Feeble Darkness	2	Stagnant Space	2
Almighty Darkness	4	Strong Initiative	3
Sleeping Darkness	2	Lasting Daze	3
Looming Darkness	4	Calm Bounty	0
Premium Room	1	Guarded Trove	2
White Room	0	False Bounty	2
Black Room	0	Moment's Reprieve	1
Martial Waking	3	Moogle Room	0
Sorcerous Waking	3	Mingling Worlds	0

Keep the following concepts in mind when choosing a map card to open a door. First, decide what type of room you want to create. If you are opening a room that leads to a story room that might contain a boss, you may want to create a room with a save point. If you are in need of battle experience or more map cards, then you'll want to create rooms with lots of Heartless. In the early stages of the game, the Waking map cards help to supplement decks with lower numbered cards. On the higher-level floors, cards like Strong Initiative or Lasting Daze provide an advantage over stronger Heartless. For more information on the different map cards and the types of rooms they create, check out the Cards chapter.

You can manage your map cards from the map card screen. To throw one away, select the type of card, then move the cursor over to the number of the card you want to delete and press the A button.

Second, keep the door requirements of the special rooms in mind. If you know that one of the special rooms requires that you use a specific numbered card (e.g. you need a #9 red map card), don't use your last one to open the door to a regular room. Alternatively, don't run up the door requirements for regular rooms too early in your trip through a world by choosing cards with higher number values than are required.

Ultimately, though, the map card you choose is largely going to be determined by what's in your inventory. Once you reach the limit of 99 cards, don't be afraid to prune your inventory, throwing out cards that you have too many of or that you never use.

TREASURE EVERYWHERE!

As you explore the rooms in Castle Oblivion, look out for any object that you can jump on or hit with Sora's Keyblade. Many of these objects release treasure that is guaranteed to be of use. The most common treasure takes the form of green and red prizes. The green HP prizes heal battle-weary bodies, while the red Moogle Points prizes provide Sora with the Moogle Points needed to buy new cards in Moogle Rooms. On occasion, a card might pop out from these treasure objects. Grab it quick before it disappears!

The best thing about Treasure Spots is that they reset each time you leave and return to a room, so you can harvest as much treasure as you have the time and patience for.

Some Treasure Spots are easier to trigger than others. If you trigger a Treasure Spot with Sora's Keyblade and it doesn't spit anything out, try jumping on top of it. Of course, it just might not have any treasure inside it!

TREASURE SPOT ITEM LOCATIONS AND PROBABILITIES

Item Name	Traverse Town	Agrabah	Olympus Coliseum	Wonderland	Monstro	Halloween Town	Atlantica	Never Land	Hollow Bastion	100 Acre Wood	Twilight Town	Destiny Islands	Castle Oblivion
Kingdom Key	50.0%	30.0%	20.0%	30.0%	30.0%	30.0%	20.0%	20.0%	20.0%	-	15.0%	10.0%	5.0%
Three Wishes	-	20.0%	-	-	-	-	-	-	-	-	-	-	-
Crabclaw	-	-	-	-	-	-	20.0%	-	-	-	-	-	-
Pumpkinhead	-	-	-	-	-	20.0%	-	-	-	-	-	-	-
Fairy Harp	-	-	-	-	-	-	-	20.0%	-	-	-	-	-
Wishing Star	-	-	-	-	20.0%	-	-	-	-	-	-	-	-
Spellbinder	-	-	-	-	-	-	-	-	-	-	-	-	-
Metal Chocobo	-	-	10.0%	-	-	-	2.0%	2.0%	2.0%	-	15.0%	-	10.0%
Olympia	-	-	20.0%	-	-	-	-	-	-	-	-	-	-
Lionheart	12.0%	-	-	-	-	-	5.0%	5.0%	5.0%	-	15.0%	-	10.0%
Lady Luck	-	-	-	20.0%	-	-	-	-	-	-	-	-	10.0%
Divine Rose	-	-	-	-	-	-	-	-	20.0%	-	-	-	-
Oathkeeper	-	-	-	-	-	-	-	-	-	-	-	15.0%	-
Oblivion	-	-	-	-	-	-	-	-	-	-	-	15.0%	-
Ultima Weapon	3.0%	3.0%	3.0%	3.0%	3.0%	3.0%	3.0%	3.0%	3.0%	-	3.0%	3.0%	3.0%
Diamond Dust	-	-	-	-	-	-	-	-	-	-	-	-	-
One-Winged Angel	-	-	-	-	-	-	-	-	-	-	5.0%	-	10.0%
Fire	10.0%	5.0%	5.0%	6.0%	5.0%	6.0%	10.0%	-	-	-	1.0%	8.0%	-
Blizzard	-	5.0%	5.0%	6.0%	5.0%	6.0%	-	10.0%	-	-	1.0%	8.0%	-
Thunder	-	-	-	-	-	-	10.0%	10.0%	10.0%	-	1.0%	8.0%	-
Cure	10.0%	-	5.0%	-	5.0%	6.0%	-	-	-	-	1.0%	-	8.0%
Gravity	-	10.0%	5.0%	5.0%	5.0%	6.0%	5.0%	5.0%	5.0%	-	1.0%	-	-
Stop	-	5.0%	5.0%	10.0%	5.0%	6.0%	5.0%	5.0%	5.0%	-	1.0%	8.0%	-
Aero	-	-	-	-	-	-	10.0%	10.0%	10.0%	-	1.0%	8.0%	-

Item Name	Traverse Town	Agrabah	Olympus Coliseum	Wonderland	Monstro	Halloween Town	Atlantica	Never Land	Hollow Bastion	100 Acre Wood	Twilight Town	Destiny Islands	Castle Oblivion
Simba	5.0%	-	-	-	-	-	-	-	-	-	1.0%	-	5.0%
Genie	-	7.0%	-	-	-	-	-	-	-	-	1.0%	-	5.0%
Bambi	-	-	-	-	-	-	-	-	-	-	1.0%	-	5.0%
Dumbo	-	-	-	-	7.0%	-	-	-	-	-	1.0%	-	5.0%
Tinker Bell	-	-	-	-	-	-	-	10.0%	-	-	1.0%	-	5.0%
Mushu	-	-	-	-	-	-	-	-	10.0%	-	1.0%	-	5.0%
Cloud	-	-	10.0%	-	-	-	-	-	-	-	1.0%	-	5.0%
Potion	10.0%	-	-	6.0%	5.0%	7.0%	3.0%	-	-	-	-	-	-
Hi-Potion	-	5.0%	7.0%	7.0%	5.0%	5.0%	4.0%	-	-	-	-	3.0%	1.0%
Mega-Potion	-	-	-	-	-	-	-	-	-	-	3.0%	-	-
Ether	-	10.0%	5.0%	7.0%	5.0%	5.0%	3.0%	-	-	-	5.0%	3.0%	1.0%
Mega-Ether	-	-	-	-	-	-	-	-	-	-	5.0%	-	2.0%
Elixir	-	-	-	-	-	-	-	-	-	-	-	3.0%	5.0%
Megalixir	-	-	-	-	-	-	-	-	-	-	-	-	-

The other great treasure-hunting location is in the Calm Bounty series of rooms. Rooms created with the Calm Bounty, Guarded Trove, and False Bounty cards contain a single treasure chest with a special treasure inside. In every world (except Traverse Town), there is at least one special battle card or sleight programmed to pop out of a chest in the first Calm Bounty-type room opened. Some worlds have two special treasures, so it is always a good idea to open another Calm Bounty-type room just in case!

After acquiring the special treasure(s) for that world, each time you open another Calm Bounty-type room, the treasure chest issues a random item. The following table lists the contents in a particular world and the probability that a certain treasure will pop out of the chest.

Learned Fire Raid!

From the second floor onward, always open at least one Calm Bounty room per world to make sure you get all the latest battle cards and sleights.

TREASURE CHEST ITEM LOCATIONS AND PROBABILITIES

Item Name	Traverse Town	Agrabah	Olympus Coliseum	Wonderland	Monstro	Halloween Town	Atlantica	Never Land	Hollow Bastion	100 Acre Wood	Twilight Town	Destiny Islands	Castle Oblivion
Kingdom Key	10.0%	-	-	-	-	-	-	-	-	-	-	-	-
Three Wishes	-	15.0%	-	-	-	-	-	-	-	-	-	-	-
Crabclaw	-	-	-	-	-	-	15.0%	-	-	-	-	-	-
Pumpkinhead	-	-	-	-	-	15.0%	-	-	-	-	-	-	-
Fairy Harp	-	-	-	-	15.0%	-	-	-	-	-	-	-	-
Wishing Star	-	-	-	-	-	-	5.0%	5.0%	5.0%	-	5.0%	-	5.0%
Spellbinder	-	-	-	-	-	-	-	-	-	-	-	-	5.0%
Metal Chocobo	-	-	5.0%	-	-	-	-	-	-	-	-	-	-
Olympia	-	-	10.0%	-	-	-	5.0%	5.0%	5.0%	-	5.0%	-	5.0%
Lionheart	10.0%	-	-	-	-	-	5.0%	5.0%	5.0%	-	5.0%	-	5.0%
Lady Luck	-	-	-	15.0%	-	-	-	-	15.0%	-	-	-	-
Divine Rose	-	-	-	-	-	-	-	-	-	-	-	10.0%	-
Oathkeeper	-	-	-	-	-	-	-	-	-	-	-	10.0%	-
Oblivion	-	-	-	-	-	-	5.0%	5.0%	5.0%	-	5.0%	5.0%	5.0%
Ultima Weapon	5.0%	5.0%	5.0%	5.0%	5.0%	5.0%	5.0%	5.0%	5.0%	-	-	-	10.0%
Diamond Dust	-	-	-	-	-	-	-	-	-	-	10.0%	-	-
One-Winged Angel	-	-	-	-	-	-	-	-	-	-	15.0%	-	10.0%
Fire	30.0%	15.0%	15.0%	15.0%	15.0%	15.0%	5.0%	5.0%	-	-	15.0%	-	10.0%
Blizzard	-	15.0%	15.0%	15.0%	15.0%	20.0%	5.0%	5.0%	10.0%	-	15.0%	-	10.0%
Thunder	-	-	-	-	-	-	20.0%	10.0%	10.0%	-	15.0%	5.0%	5.0%
Cure	30.0%	5.0%	5.0%	5.0%	5.0%	5.0%	-	10.0%	10.0%	-	-	20.0%	5.0%
Gravity	-	20.0%	10.0%	-	10.0%	10.0%	-	10.0%	10.0%	-	-	20.0%	5.0%
Stop	-	-	10.0%	20.0%	10.0%	10.0%	10.0%	-	10.0%	-	-	20.0%	5.0%
Aero	-	-	-	-	-	-	20.0%	10.0%	10.0%	-	-	-	-
Simba	10.0%	-	-	5.0%	-	5.0%	-	-	-	-	-	-	-
Genie	-	15.0%	-	-	-	-	-	-	-	-	5.0%	-	-
Bambi	-	-	-	-	-	-	10.0%	-	-	-	-	-	-
Dumbo	-	-	-	-	15.0%	-	-	-	-	-	-	-	-
Tinker Bell	-	-	-	-	-	-	-	20.0%	-	-	-	-	-
Mushu	-	-	-	-	-	-	-	-	20.0%	-	-	-	-
Cloud	-	-	15.0%	-	-	-	-	-	-	-	-	-	-
Potion	5.0%	-	-	10.0%	-	5.0%	-	5.0%	-	-	-	-	-
Hi-Potion	-	-	-	10.0%	5.0%	5.0%	-	-	-	-	10.0%	-	5.0%
Mega-Potion	-	-	-	-	-	-	-	-	5.0%	-	-	-	-
Ether	-	10.0%	-	-	5.0%	5.0%	-	-	-	-	-	-	10.0%
Mega-Ether	-	-	-	-	-	-	-	-	-	-	-	5.0%	3.0%
Elixir	-	-	-	-	-	-	-	-	-	-	-	-	2.0%
Megalixir	-	-	-	-	-	-	-	-	-	-	-	-	-

Another source of treasure is the Moogle Shop. When you use a Moogle Room card to open a door, it creates a room populated by a single moogle merchant. This merchant is more than willing to sell new packs of cards and buy your old and unused ones. The currency used in this shop is the Moogle Point, which is issued from Treasure Spots in the form of Moogle Points drops. Since Treasure Spots reset whenever you exit a room, you can go back to any Treasure Spot throughout the world to gather enough Moogle Points to buy out the shop.

Your first visit to the Moogle Shop always begins with a free pack of cards. This is reason enough to open at least one shop per world!

Combo Packs include all three types of battle cards, making them a great purchase if you are on a budget. However, with the availability of Moogle Points from the Treasure Spots, budget should not be an issue.

Moogle Shops sell cards in packs of five. There are four different types of packs: attack cards, magic cards, item cards, and a Combo Pack. The contents of each pack are randomly chosen according to the probabilities listed in the following table.

As you proceed further in the Castle, packs of cards with higher rarity cards start to appear inside Moogle Shops. These packs are more expensive, but worth it if you get a rare card that you really need.

TYPES OF CARD PACKS

Belt Color	Card Rarity	Availability	Price			
			Attack Pack	Magic Pack	Item Pack	Combo Pack
Green Leaf	Low	1F-13F	100 Moogle Points	200 Moogle Points	150 Moogle Points	150 Moogle Points
Brown Belt	Medium	7F-13F	200 Moogle Points	250 Moogle Points	200 Moogle Points	200 Moogle Points
Black Belt	High	7F-13F	300 Moogle Points	270 Moogle Points	300 Moogle Points	300 Moogle Points
Moogle Belt	Supreme	11F-13F	500 Moogle Points	300 Moogle Points	350 Moogle Points	400 Moogle Points

MOOGLE SHOP CARD LIST PROBABILITIES

Card Name	Pack 1	Pack 2	Pack 3	Pack 4
Kingdom Key	-	-	-	-
Three Wishes	20%	14%	4%	4%
Crabclaw	20%	14%	4%	4%
Pumpkinhead	20%	14%	4%	4%
Fairy Harp	20%	14%	4%	4%
Wishing Star	20%	14%	4%	4%
Spellbinder	-	5%	10%	6%
Metal Chocobo	-	5%	10%	6%
Olympia	-	5%	10%	6%
Lionheart	-	5%	10%	6%
Lady Luck	-	5%	10%	6%
Divine Rose	-	5%	10%	6%
Oathkeeper	-	-	5%	10%
Oblivion	-	-	5%	10%
Ultima Weapon	-	-	5%	10%
Diamond Dust	-	-	5%	10%
One-Winged Angel	-	-	-	4%
Fire	15%	10%	5%	5%
Blizzard	15%	10%	5%	5%
Thunder	15%	10%	5%	5%
Cure	-	5%	10%	5%
Gravity	-	5%	10%	5%
Stop	-	5%	10%	5%
Aero	10%	5%	-	-
Simba	20%	5%	5%	5%
Genie	10%	20%	8%	10%

MOOGLE SHOP CARD LIST PROBABILITIES (CON'T.)

Card Name	Pack 1	Pack 2	Pack 3	Pack 4
Bambi	-	-	8%	10%
Dumbo	10%	20%	8%	10%
Tinker Bell	-	-	8%	10%
Mushu	-	-	8%	10%
Cloud	5%	5%	10%	15%
Potion	50%	40%	-	-
Hi-Potion	50%	40%	20%	15%
Mega-Potion	-	10%	25%	20%
Ether	-	10%	25%	20%
Mega-Ether	-	-	15%	20%
Elixir	-	-	15%	15%
Megalixir	-	-	-	10%

PROBABILITIES FOR CARD NUMBERS

Card Value	%	Card Value	%
0	5%	5	10%
1	15%	6	10%
2	15%	7	6%
3	16%	8	5%
4	14%	9	4%

The great thing about Moogle Shops is that they are an easy way to build a powerful deck quickly and early in the game. They are also great places to dispose of cards that you may not use. Simply go over to the moogle on the right side of the shop screen and sell him your unwanted cards. You can then turn around and use the profits to buy new cards. Moogle Shops are also great places to find premium cards.

WELCOME TO CASTLE OBLIVION

CHARACTERS

GAME BASICS

CASTLE OBLIVION

SECRETS OF THE GAME

THE CARDS

BESTIARY

CHANGING ROOMS, REVISITING WORLDS, AND CHOOSING YOUR PATH

If you aren't satisfied with the rooms you've already opened in a world for one reason or another, you can recreate the world by opening it with another map card. This is handier than you might think. Recreating rooms replenishes rooms with Heartless if you need to level up before taking on a boss. If you've created a lot of small rooms with few Treasure Spots and you need Moogle Points to buy card packs, you can recreate them with cards that produce larger rooms with more Treasure Spots. Also, it is a good idea to save the creation of Moment's Reprieve rooms, which contain save points, and Moogle Rooms until after you've opened up all of the regular rooms and killed off all of the Heartless. This enables you to maximize your leveling up opportunities before you create rooms that have no Heartless to defeat.

Once you leave a world and open another, the rooms in the last world you visited are erased. If you need to return to that world for any reason, simply find a warp point in the hallway to the entrance of the world you are currently in. Warp points instantly take you back to the entrance of the world you want to revisit.

Save points are diamond-shaped, while warp points are spherical in shape. You'll find one of each in the hallway right before the entrance to a world.

And speaking of leaving and entering worlds, on Floors 2-6 and 7-10 you get to choose the world you want to enter for each floor. This guide's walkthrough is based upon the default world for each floor, but you are encouraged to make your own decisions when it comes to that choice. Use the maps and information contained in the walkthrough to determine which world you think is most appropriate for each floor. Since all of the game's treasures are allocated to the world, you won't miss out on anything.

A battle begins whenever Sora touches one of the Heartless on the field. If a Heartless touches Sora first, the battle begins normally, but if Sora hits the Heartless with his Keyblade, the Heartless start the battle in a stunned state, which means you can attack unhindered. Battles play a large role in this game, so it is important that you become proficient in the art of card battling as soon as possible.

BASICS OF THE FIGHT

As you proceed through Traverse Town on the first floor of Castle Oblivion, plenty of people will give advice on the game's battle system. Theory is good, but the best way to gain proficiency is through experience. Defeat all of the Heartless in the rooms you create until you feel comfortable with the Card Battle system.

Basically, the system works as follows: You start the game with a basic card deck that contains attack cards, a magic card, and an item card. There is a fourth class of card, the enemy card, but you'll need to fight a few battles (or defeat the boss in Traverse Town) to acquire one of them. The five classes of battle cards are as follows:

 Attack Cards: This class is comprised of the different Keyblades that Sora can use in battle. Each attack card has its own strengths and weaknesses, so check out its stats before you place new cards into your deck.

 Magic Cards: This class is comprised of both magic and summoning cards. Magic cards enable you to cast the standard spells, including Fire, Blizzard, Thunder, Cure, and so on. Summon cards enable you to call a friend into battle.

 Friend Cards: This class of cards is very similar to the summon cards in the Magic category. However, friend cards only appear during battles. Which friend cards appear in battle is determined by who you have in your party in any given world. Donald Duck and Goofy fill the first two slots in every world except Destiny Islands. The third slot is filled if you are in a world where you have a friend willing to help out.

 Item Cards: Item cards are used to reload used cards and even reset the reload counter. These cards can only be used once in battle.

 Enemy Cards: Enemy cards appear on a separate Card Reel and are accessed by pressing the SELECT button during battle. These cards trigger unusual effects or grant Sora special powers.

Each card is assigned a number from 0 to 9. In battle, you play your cards and your foes play theirs. Each card is equivalent to an action: attack cards trigger Keyblade attacks and magic cards cause Sora to cast the corresponding magic spell. An attack is considered successful if the numerical value of your card surpasses that of your enemy, or if you play a card and the attack ends before the enemy plays a card of his own. An attack fails if you play a card with a numerical value less than that of the card your enemy currently has in play or if you play a card and then your enemy counters with a card with a higher number afterwards.

That is the theory behind the system. When you are in battle, it feels like a normal RPG-style battle. You still play in real-time and you still have to chase down the enemy, aim your attack, and so on. The only difference is that the success or failure of your attacks is determined by the cards played.

The main strategy in the Card Battle system is a little thing called "card breaking." A card break occurs when you play a card that has a higher value than the card your opponent has already played. For example, if the Shadow you are fighting plays an attack card with the value of 8, you would need to play a 9 card or a zero card to cause a card break to end his attack. Continuing to play cards with lower numbers does nothing to stop his attack and, in effect, just wastes the cards, which are deflected into the reload pile.

Of all the cards, the most powerful are the 9 card and zero cards. 9 cards have the honor of being almost impossible to break by themselves, making them the card to use if you plan to use a lot of magic or item cards (more on the item cards later). The only way you can card break a 9 card is with a combo or with the zero card.

The zero card is quite fascinating. On one hand, it has the power to card break any card in play—including combinations and sleights! On the other hand, its value is 0 and, as such, can be broken by any card, even a 1! As you collect more cards and start to customize decks for the harder battles on the upper floors of Castle Oblivion, you'll want quite a few zero cards in your deck. However, don't base an entire deck around them!

When you run out of cards, the only thing that remains is the blank "reload" card. Press and hold down the A button to recharge and reload your deck. The number that appears on the reload card is the reload counter and it indicates the number of times the reload gauge must charge before your deck is reloaded and you can resume your offense. The maximum number of recharge passes is three, but it is possible to reset that with the help of item cards. During the time you are holding down the A Button, you cannot move or continue to attack. If you sustain damage while reloading your deck, the operation is interrupted while Sora recovers from the blow.

You can only reload cards that are marked as "reloadable." A card is considered "unreloadable" if it was card broken in the previous round, used as the starting card of a sleight, or if it is a premium card. Unreloadable cards can only be resurrected by certain item cards.

ADVANCED TACTICS: COMBO ATTACKS

You also have the option of playing multiple cards at a time. To stock cards for use in a combo, press both the L and R Buttons at the same time and the card at the top of your deck moves to the top left of the screen. You can produce two- and three-card combinations. Combo attacks are performed as consecutive attacks unless the cards chosen fit the criteria for a sleight. The value of a combo attack is the sum of the three cards. To card break a combo, you must play a card or another combo with a higher value. Alternatively, you can just play a zero card.

Sleights are special attacks that Sora learns as he makes his way through Castle Oblivion. These attacks combine specific cards to create powerful attacks with amazing effects. The following table lists the card requirements for each sleight, its effects, how to learn it, and how it affects certain types of enemies.

WELCOME TO
CASTLE OBLIVION

CHARACTERS

GAME BASICS

CASTLE OBLIVION

SECRETS OF
THE GAME

THE CARDS

BESTIARY

Name	How to Activate	Effect	How to Obtain	Effect vs. Heartless	Effect vs. Heartless Bosses	Effect vs. Human Bosses
Sliding Dash	Same type of attack cards, value 10-15	Slide toward distant targets for a close-range attack.	After level 2	0	0	0
Stun Impact	Same type of attack cards, value 20-23	Stun surrounding enemies with a single attack.	After level 7	0	×	×
Strike Raid	3 attack cards with value 24-26	Hurl the Keyblade forward, stunning and dealing damage.	After level 12	0	0	0
Blitz	Different type of attack cards, value 10-15	Unleash a powerful three-hit combo upon the enemy.	After level 17	0	0	0
Sonic Blade	Different type of attack cards, value 20-23	Rocket across the field, striking down any enemies in the way. Press the A Button for up to six additional attacks.	After level 22	0	0	0
Zantetsuken	3 attack cards with value 0 or 27	Break a card and render it unreloadable until the end of the battle.	After level 27	×	×	0
Ars Arcanum	3 attack cards with value 1-6	Rain a flurry of blows upon the enemy.	After level 37	0	0	0
Ragnarok	3 attack cards, value 7-9	Leap into the air and fire a stream of rays in front of you.	After level 47	0	0	0
Trinity Limit	Attack + Donald + Goofy	Inflict heavy damage on all enemies in sight.	Event at the start entrance on 13F.	0	0	0
Fira	2 Fire	Sizzle the opposition with powerful fire magic.	After obtaining the first magic card for this magic.	0	0	0
Firaga	3 Fire	Scorch the opposition with supreme fire magic.	After obtaining the first magic card for this magic.	0	0	0
Blizzara	2 Blizzard	Chill the opposition with powerful ice magic.	After obtaining the first magic card for this magic.	0	0	0
Blizzaga	3 Blizzard	Freeze the opposition with supreme ice magic.	After obtaining the first magic card for this magic.	0	0	0
Thundara	2 Thunder	Shock the opposition with powerful lightning magic.	After obtaining the first magic card for this magic.	0	0	0
Thundaga	3 Thunder	Fry the opposition with supreme lightning magic.	After obtaining the first magic card for this magic.	0	0	0
Cura	2 Cure	Restore a lot of HP.	After obtaining the first magic card for this magic.	0	0	0
Curaga	3 Cure	Restore a very large amount of HP.	After obtaining the first magic card for this magic.	0	0	0
Gravira	2 Gravity	Deal damage relative to the enemy's remaining HP.	After obtaining the first magic card for this magic.	0	×	×
Graviga	3 Gravity	Deal damage relative to the enemy's remaining HP.	After obtaining the first magic card for this magic.	0	×	×
Stopra	2 Stop	Halt enemy movement for a long period of time.	After obtaining the first magic card for this magic.	0	×	×
Stopga	3 Stop	Halt enemy movement for a long period of time.	After obtaining the first magic card for this magic.	0	×	×
Aerora	2 Aero	Blow away surrounding enemies and inflict damage.	After obtaining the first magic card for this magic.	0	0	0
Aeroga	3 Aero	Blow away all enemies in a large radius and inflict damage.	After obtaining the first magic card for this magic.	0	0	0
Aqua Splash	Blizzard + Fire + Aero	Spray melted ice at the enemy over a period of time, inflicting ice damage.	Treasure Chest in Key to Rewards Room at Monstro.	0	0	0
Bind	Gravity + Stop + Magic	Hold enemies in place. Enemies can still attack from their positions.	After the event with Eeyore at 100 Acre Wood.	0	×	0
Blizzard Raid	Blizzard + Attack + Attack	Hurl the Keyblade and inflict ice damage.	Treasure Chest created in Calm Bounty-type room in Olympus Coliseum.	0	0	0
Confuse	Genie + Tinker Bell + Summon	Temporarily confuse enemies so they attack less often.	After the event with Piglet at 100 Acre Wood.	0	×	×
Firaga Break	Fire + Mushu + Attack	Inflict fire damage on enemies in front of you with a powerful attack.	Treasure Chest created in Calm Bounty-type room in Twilight Town.	0	0	0
Fire Raid	Fire + Attack + Attack	Hurl the Keyblade and inflict fire damage.	Treasure Chest created in Calm Bounty-type room in Monstro.	0	0	0
Gifted Miracle	Summon + Magic + Jack Bambi + Blizzard + Item	Reload cards and reset the counter while restoring HP to friends and foes alike.	Treasure Chest created in Calm Bounty-type rooms in Agrabah.	0	0	0
Gravity Raid	Gravity + Attack + Attack	Hurl the Keyblade and trigger Gravity upon impact.	Treasure Chest in Key to Rewards Room at Halloween Town.	0	×	×
Holy	Mega-Ether + Megalixir + Item	Inflict damage on a targeted enemy and all surrounding enemies.	After level 42.	0	0	0
Homing Blizzara	Aero + Blizzard + Magic	Cast a Blizzara spell that seeks out the targeted enemy.	Treasure Chest created in second Calm Bounty-type rooms in Atlantica.	0	0	0
Homing Fira	Aero + Fire + Magic	Cast a Fire spell that seeks out the targeted enemy.	Treasure Chest created in second Calm Bounty-type rooms in Never Land.	0	0	0

Name	How to Activate	Effect	How to Obtain	Effect vs. Heartless	Effect vs. Heartless Bosses	Effect vs. Human Bosses
Judgment	Aero + Attack + Attack	Hurl the Keyblade toward the enemy for multiple attacks.	Treasure Chest created in Calm Bounty-type rooms in Destiny Islands.	0	0	0
Mega Flare	Mushu + Fire + Fire	Incinerate all enemies in a wide area.	After level 52.	0	0	0
Quake	Gravity + Simba + Magic	Inflict damage on all ground enemies with a violent tremor.	Treasure Chest in Key to Rewards Room at Atlantica.	0	0	0
Reflect Raid	Cloud + Attack + Attack	Hurl the Keyblade and make it ricochet around to strike many enemies.	Treasure Chest created in second Calm Bounty-type rooms in Hollow Bastion.	0	0	0
Shock Impact	Simba + Attack + Attack	Simba's roar sends enemies flying and triggers Stop.	Treasure Chest created in Calm Bounty-type room in Atlantica.	0	×	×
Stop Raid	Stop + Attack + Attack	Hurl the Keyblade and trigger Stop upon impact.	Treasure Chest in Key to Rewards Room at Wonderland.	0	×	×
Synchro	Cure + Gravity + Aero	Set surrounding enemies' HP to that of the target.	After the event with Rabbit at 100 Acre Wood.	0	×	×
Teleport	Magic + Magic + Peter Pan / Stop + Aero + Item	Rematerialize behind the targeted enemy, stunning it for a short time.	Treasure Chest created in first Calm Bounty-type rooms in Never Land.	0	×	×
Terror	Summon + Summon + Jack / Simba + Mushu + Item	Strike fear in the enemy so they no longer approach.	After the start event at Halloween Town.	0	×	×
Thunder Raid	Thunder + Attack + Attack	Hurl the Keyblade and inflict lightning damage.	Treasure Chest in Key to Rewards Room at Never Land.	0	0	0
Tornado	Aero + Gravity + Summon	Blow away enemies in a wide area, inflicting damage and stunning them.	After level 32.	0	0	0
Warp	Stop + Aero + Aero	Eliminate all enemies in sight.	Treasure Chest in Key to Rewards Room at Twilight Town.	0	×	×
Warpinator	Stop + Gravity + Aero	Eliminate the closest enemy. Not always successful.	Defeat Riku Replica at goal entrance on 8F.	0	×	×
Blazing Donald	Fire + Donald + Magic	Donald flubs a Fire spell...	Treasure Chest in Key to Rewards Room at Agrabah.	0	0	0
Cross-slash	2 Cloud	Cloud assaults the enemy with a three-hit combo.	After obtaining the first magic card for this magic.	0	0	0
Ferocious Lunge	2 The Beast	The Beast charges in a straight line, scattering the opposition.	Available while this character is in your party.	0	0	–
Ferocious Lunge	3 The Beast	The Beast charges in a straight line, crushing the opposition.	Available while this character is in your party.	0	0	–
Flare Breath	2 Mushu	Mushu breathes fire at enemies in a wide area, inflicting fire damage.	After obtaining the first magic card for this magic.	0	0	0
Flare Breath	3 Mushu	Mushu breathes even more fire at enemies in a wide area, inflicting fire damage.	After obtaining the first magic card for this magic.	0	0	0
Goofy Charge	2 Goofy	Goofy rushes at enemies, bashing and stunning them with his shield.	Default	0	0	0
Goofy Tornado	3 Goofy	Goofy whirls his shield around, bashing enemies in a wide area.	Default	0	0	0
Hummingbird	2 Peter Pan	Peter Pan soars around, striking enemies in a wide area.	Available while this character is in your party.	0	0	0
Hummingbird	3 Peter Pan	Peter Pan soars around for an even longer time, striking enemies in a wide area.	Available while this character is in your party.	0	0	0
Idyll Romp	Bambi + Attack + Attack	Bambi zigzags around the battlefield, confusing the enemy.	After the event with Tigger in 100 Acre Wood.	0	×	×
Magic	2 Donald	Donald double-casts Fira, Blizzara, Thundara or Cura.	Default	0	0	0
Magic	3 Goofy	Donald double-casts Firaga, Blizzaga, Thundaga or Curaga.	Default	0	0	0
Omnislash	3 Cloud	Cloud swoops down from the skies, attacking enemies in a wide area.	After obtaining the first magic card for this magic.	0	0	0
	Cloud + Stop + Attack	Cloud swoops down from the skies, attacking enemies in a wide area.	Treasure Chest created in first Calm Bounty-type rooms in Hollow Bastion.	0	0	0
Paradise	2 Bambi	Bambi bounds around and drops HP recovery items.	After obtaining the first magic card for this magic.	0	0	0
Paradise	3 Bambi	Bambi bounds around and drops HP recovery items while stunning the enemy.	After obtaining the first magic card for this magic.	0	0	0
Proud Roar	2 Simba	Simba's roar stuns and deals damage to enemies in front of him.	After obtaining the first magic card for this magic.	0	0	0
Proud Roar	3 Simba	Simba's roar stuns and deals even more damage to enemies in front of him.	After obtaining the first magic card for this magic.	0	0	0
Sandstorm	2 Aladdin	Aladdin runs around while swinging his sword.	Available while this character is in your party.	0	0	–
Sandstorm	3 Aladdin	Aladdin runs around for a longer period of time while swinging his sword.	Available while this character is in your party.	0	0	–
Showtime	2 Genie	Genie randomly casts two spells chosen from Gravira, Thundara and Stopga.	After obtaining the first magic card for this magic.	0	0	–
Showtime	3 Genie	Genie randomly casts three spells chosen from Gravira, Thundara and Stopra.	After obtaining the first magic card for this magic.	0	0	0
Spiral Wave	2 Ariel	Ariel whirls back and forth, striking many enemies.	Available while this character is in your party.	0	0	–
Spiral Wave	3 Ariel	Ariel whirls back and forth, striking many enemies for an even longer time.	Available while this character is in your party.	0	0	–
Splash	2 Dumbo	Dumbo douses enemies over a set time period, dealing ice damage.	After obtaining the first magic card for this magic.	0	0	0
Splash	3 Dumbo	Dumbo douses enemies in a wide area for a set time period, dealing ice damage.	After obtaining the first magic card for this magic.	0	0	0
Surprise!	2 Jack	Jack double-casts Fira, Blizzara, Thundara or Gravira.	Available while this character is in your party.	0	0	0
Surprise!	3 Jack	Jack triple-casts Firaga, Blizzaga, Thundaga or Gravira.	Available while this character is in your party.	0	0	–
Twinkle	2 Tinker Bell	Tinker Bell restores a lot of HP over a set time period.	After obtaining the first magic card for this magic.	–	–	–
Twinkle	3 Tinker Bell	Tinker Bell restores a very large amount of HP over an extended time period.	After obtaining the first magic card for this magic.	–	–	–

BUILDING A STRONG DECK

Of course, the best way to win battles is with a great deck. After fighting a few battles and leveling up a bit, start thinking about expanding the deck you start the game with. To modify your deck, choose the Review Decks option on the Main Menu screen. You can create up to three decks, but for the majority of the game, you'll probably only use one or two of those slots.

The walkthrough in this guide provides advice on how to customize your deck for optimum results in battle, but you should always feel free to experiment and come up with your own strategies. If you like to use magic, then build your deck around various magic cards. If you are more of a hack and slash person, then pack your deck full of attack cards.

The Review Decks screen is where all of the micro-management takes place!

Here are some general suggestions to keep in mind:

1. Consider creating a deck for both normal battles and boss battles. Each type requires different strategies and separate decks are easier to deal with compared to recreating a deck each time you enter or leave an area with a boss.

2. Open and buy out at least one Moogle Shop on each floor. If you have the time and patience, open and buy out two. This will provide plenty of cards and it will enable you to experiment with different sleights, card combinations, and deck constructions.

3. Dispose of any weak attack cards every four or five floors. The amount of damage caused by attack cards is determined by the Keyblade's stats, so it makes sense to replace weaker cards with stronger ones.

4. By the time you reach the seventh floor, make sure the value of your cards is around 7 or above. By the time you reach the upper floors, you'll want your deck to consist largely of 9 cards, with a certain percentage of zero cards to card break dangerous sleights.

5. To aid in building a deck, boost Sora's CP (Card Points) twice for every HP Boost. The more CP, the more cards you can use in a deck.

6. Clearing your deck of cards and starting from scratch is a great way to take stock of your card inventory and try new arrangements.

7. If you are fond of using sleights, arrange your deck accordingly. Placing the cards needed to create your favorite sleights right by each other only makes sense and it prevents you from having to waste time scrolling through the Card Reel searching for the right card.

8. Tuck zero cards where you think you might need them in the course of a battle. Put one or two at the start of your deck, then scroll by them when the battle starts. When you need one, simply press the R Button and it's at the start of your deck ready to be played.

9. Always take your healing needs into consideration when creating a deck. Keeping two or three high-numbered Cure cards at the end of a deck for boss battles is always helpful. In regular battles, one or two should suffice. Also, don't forget that healing comes from unusual sources, like summon and friend cards!

10. Lastly, think about ending a deck with a high-numbered item card or two. If you stock a large quantity of attack cards in a deck, go with Potions or Hi-Potions to aid in quickly reloading the cards you need the most. If you are a fan of magic cards, use Ether cards instead.

WELCOME TO CASTLE OBLIVION

CHARACTERS

GAME BASICS

CASTLE OBLIVION

SECRETS OF THE GAME

THE CARDS

BESTIARY

CASTLE OBLIVION, FIRST FLOOR

After meeting your host, you receive your first world card. Use the world card on the entrance to the first floor to recreate Traverse Town in the rooms of the castle. Where you can go in Traverse Town is determined by the floor's blueprint. Since you can't choose your destination on this floor, this section will discuss both the first floor and Traverse Town together. From the second floor to the tenth floor, you get to choose the world you want to visit from a list. At that point, the specifics about the floor and the "featured" world will be discussed separately.

FEATURED WORLD

To clear Traverse Town and progress to the second floor, you must visit the three "story" rooms on the World Map. These rooms are shaded yellow on the World Map and can only be opened once you have a specific Keycard in your possession. They are called "story" rooms because the storyline behind each world is played out inside during cut-scenes. In Traverse Town, the characters you meet in the story rooms provide a tutorial on battle specifics and a little bit of background to the game. In the third story room, you must defeat the game's first boss—but more on that a bit later!

WORLD MAP

FIRST FLOOR

TRAVERSE TOWN

LUGGAGE

DRESS & SUIT

To Castle
Oblivion
Main Hall

MAP INFORMATION!

This map is a sample map of Traverse Town. This map was created using all Tranquil Darkness cards. While the rooms you create might not look the same as the ones here, the special door requirements and the layout of the floorplan are identical.

Chest   Crate   Hutch   Lamppost

To
the second floor

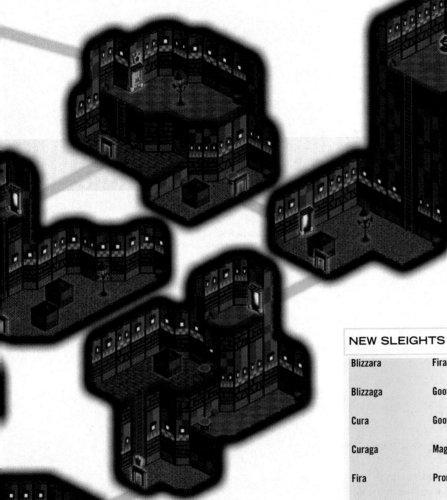

WELCOME TO
CASTLE OBLIVION

CHARACTERS

GAME BASICS

CASTLE
OBLIVION

FIRST FLOOR

SECOND FLOOR

THIRD FLOOR

FOURTH FLOOR

FIFTH FLOOR

SIXTH FLOOR

SEVENTH FLOOR

EIGHTH FLOOR

NINTH FLOOR

TENTH FLOOR

ELEVENTH FLOOR

TWELFTH FLOOR

THIRTEENTH FLOOR

SECRETS OF THE
GAME

THE CARDS

BESTIARY

NEW SLEIGHTS

Blizzara	Firaga
Blizzaga	Goofy Charge
Cura	Goofy Tornado
Curaga	Magic
Fira	Proud Roar

COMMON BATTLE CARDS

- Kingdom Key
- Blizzard
- Fire
- Cure
- Potion
- Lionheart
- Simba

COMMON MAP CARDS

- Tranquil Darkness
- Teeming Darkness
- Feeble Darkness
- Sleeping Darkness
- Meeting Ground

COMMON HEARTLESS

- Guard Armor (boss)
- Blue Rhapsody
- Shadow
- Soldier

Room Synthesis

The cards you see shall be the key—

Doors emblazoned with a crown are special doors.

You need a special Keycard to open the story rooms. There are three main Keycards: The Key of Beginnings, Key of Guidance, and the Key to Truth. These are presented at the end of cut-scenes and can only be used once. The fourth Keycard, the Key to Rewards, is randomly won at the end of battles from the seventh floor to the top of the Castle and is used to open special treasure rooms on each floor.

Leon, it's you! What are you doing in Castle Oblivion?

Upon entering a story room, a cut-scene begins. Each world has its own tale to tell and you can be sure that each story will have at least one boss to fight. After visiting a story room, it is closed off for the rest of the game.

The flow of the game established on the first floor rarely changes throughout the rest of the game, so use your time in Traverse Town to get into some good habits.

LEON

A cool and collected swordsman who wields a gunblade. His real name: Squall Leonhart. Leon once fought with Sora against the Heartless, but the Leon we met in Castle Oblivion is a product of Sora's memory, so he can't remember much of what happened before.

First, it's a good idea to open up all of the regular rooms before hitting the story rooms. This enables you to fight monsters, build up experience, and collect map and battle-related cards. You can use any of the map cards in your possession to open up a new room as long as it fulfills the opening requirements. As you'll quickly learn, some map cards offer a safer journey than others. For example, the Moment's Reprieve card creates a small room with a save point and no Heartless. The Teeming Darkness card creates a large room and is filled with aggressive enemies.

The Sleeping Darkness card creates a small room but it is filled with Heartless frozen in sleep. You can choose to battle or dodge them.

However, don't avoid rooms with lots of Heartless. Most of these rooms only spawn about an average of five groups of monsters and once you've defeated them, you can wander the room safely without fear of continued battles. If you need to fight more Heartless to get more map cards or more experience points, then you can reset a room by simply tapping on the door with Sora's Keyblade and using another map card. The only rooms that cannot be reset in this way are the story rooms and the "exit" room.

For safety's sake, stand by the door to the room as you defeat each group of Heartless. This makes it easy if you need to escape from the room to heal any wounds.

One of the benefits of clearing a room is that it makes it easier to go treasure hunting. There are certain items and geographical features in each world that expel cards, green HP prizes and red Moogle Point prizes. To get the treasure, you must either strike the object with Sora's Keyblade or jump on top of it. These Treasure Spots are reset each time you leave and re-enter a room.

In Traverse Town, wooden boxes, skylights, and lampposts hide treasure.

THE KEY TO REWARDS

Upon reaching the seventh floor, Key to Rewards cards join the list of things you get as booty at the end of a successful battle. After acquiring one, return to the first floor and use it to open the Key to Rewards room. Inside you'll find a treasure chest with the special Keyblade, *Lionheart*, inside. This is a mid-level Keyblade enchanted with the power of fire.

After opening up all of the regular rooms, it's time to head to the first story room. This is where you meet with old friends and learn some "advanced battle tactics." At the end of the cut-scene, you receive the **Key of Guidance**, which is required to open the second room. Visit the second story room and head to the third room with the Key to Truth in hand. The first boss, the Guard Armor, is inside the third story room.

SPECIAL TREASURES IN TRAVERSE TOWN

When you pick up a **Key to Rewards** card on the seventh floor or higher, return here to Traverse Town to pick up the treasure from the special Key to Rewards room: the Lionheart attack card!

BOSS BATTLE GUARD ARMOR

The Guard Armor is comprised of disjointed pieces of armor. To defeat this boss, you must destroy each piece of armor until all that remains is its head.

The best way to defeat the Guard Armor is to prevent him from launching an attack. To do so, constantly press the A Button to attack and card break. The Potion card enables you to reload all of your attack cards automatically, making it possible to go two rounds without stopping to recharge your deck.

Whether you use single attacks or combos, like the sleight Sliding Dash, keeping up your attacks prevents the Guard Armor from attacking most of the time.

As you battle the Guard Armor, keep an eye out for special trick cards (with the green Mickey Mouse logo). This card appears in much the same manner as the friend cards and allows you to disrupt the battle, causing the Guard Armor to literally fall to pieces. This card only appears during boss fights and provides a momentary advantage over the boss.

When the Guard Armor does connect with an attack, watch out for its wandering feet or fists. After destroying both hands and feet, the Guard Armor starts spinning around the room, trying to cause damage with its torso. Be very quick with your attacks and hit the Guard Armor once it enters this mode. Alternatively, you can use the trick card to stop the Guard Armor in mid-spin.

The trick card breaks the Guard Armor into pieces, making it a perfect way to disrupt the Guard Armor's spinning torso attack.

The Guard Armor's boots were certainly made for walking, and they'll stomp all over you if you aren't careful!

For defeating the Guard Armor, you receive experience prizes and the *Guard Armor card*. This enemy card, when used in battle, extends the range of your deck's attack cards for up to 30 attacks.

WELCOME TO CASTLE OBLIVION

CHARACTERS

GAME BASICS

CASTLE OBLIVION

First Floor

Second Floor

Third Floor

Fourth Floor

Fifth Floor

Sixth Floor

Seventh Floor

Eighth Floor

Ninth Floor

Tenth Floor

Eleventh Floor

Twelfth Floor

Thirteenth Floor

SECRETS OF THE GAME

THE CARDS

BESTIARY

Winning the boss fight in the third story room opens the "exit" room. This room contains a save point and the door into the hall leading to the second floor. Save the game at this point, just to be safe. This is a common ambush spot of the Organization and there's a high probability that you'll run into a bad guy aching for a fight as you head to the next floor.

AXEL

Axel seems to just be messing around... but for all we know, he's done more thinking than everyone else put together.

Perhaps YOU'D like to test him.

Even the hallways between the worlds are dangerous! Save your game in the "exit" room before leaving a world just in case an ambush awaits.

BOSS BATTLE AXEL

Before you get to the second floor, you encounter the hooded host and his friend, Axel. This battle is tougher than the Guard Armor fight because Axel has the ability to use fire (in fact, at the end of the battle, you receive your first Fire card!). His big sleight is Fire Wall, which sends a wall of fire sliding across the battlefield. There are two ways to dodge this attack: 1. Get on the other side of it when Axel casts it; or 2. Card break it. You'll know Axel is about to summon Fire Wall when he pulls a card combo up on his side of the screen. When three cards line up, get close to Axel's side or backside!

INSIDE THE BOSS'S DECK

Axel's deck consists of 14 cards. He has two types of attack cards and performs a single sleight, Fire Wall. His "A" attack card attack is a combination attack and his "B" attack card is a boomerang attack with his shuriken-like weapons. Fire Wall is created when Axel stocks three of the "A" cards.

His deck is as follows:
"A" attack cards: 0 (x1); 2 (x2); 3 (x1); 4 (x2); 6 (x1)
"B" attack cards: 1 (x2); 3 (x2); 4 (x1); 5 (x2)
No enemy or item cards.

Blizzard is a good choice against the fiery Axel, if you can get him to stand still long enough to cast the spell!

Watch out for the Fire Wall! It is very difficult to dodge unless you can card break the attack

GOOFY

Captain of the Disney Castle Royal Knights. He set out with Donald after the king's disappearance. He is cheerful and calm and no one is more loyal to the king. Goofy and Sora are especially good friends.

DONALD DUCK

Court wizard at Disney Castle who set out with Goofy after the king's disappearance. His short temper sometimes gets him into trouble, but he is very brave.

Donald is currently seeking clues to what happened to the king after he was locked behind the door of darkness.

Once you acquire more world cards, the journey continues. Which world awaits you on the second floor is entirely up to you...

For defeating Axel, you get a **Fire card** and a set of five new **world cards**. These cards are used to open up the next five floors. When you are ready to abandon the first floor, head up the steps. However, leaving a floor erases all of the rooms that you've created and cleared already. When you return to that floor, you must open and clear the rooms again. This is a great way to gain experience and collect more cards, so don't be afraid to revisit old haunts. In addition, each floor has a special Treasure room that requires the rare Key to Rewards Keycard, which is only available on the seventh floors and higher! After obtaining your first Key to Rewards card, return to Traverse Town and get the treasure inside!

WELCOME TO CASTLE OBLIVION

CHARACTERS

GAME BASICS

CASTLE OBLIVION

First Floor

Second Floor

Third Floor

Fourth Floor

Fifth Floor

Sixth Floor

Seventh Floor

Eighth Floor

Ninth Floor

Tenth Floor

Eleventh Floor

Twelfth Floor

Thirteenth Floor

SECRETS OF THE GAME

THE CARDS

BESTIARY

CASTLE OBLIVION, SECOND FLOOR

When you approach the door to the second floor, you have a choice between which of the five new world cards you can use first. Each room is unique in storyline and requires that you fight at least one boss to complete the world and progress to the next floor.

This guide is structured in a manner that chooses to go with the "default" world on each floor. The "default" room is the first one that is presented when you open the door to a new floor. For the second floor, this world card is Agrabah from the movie *Aladdin*. If you'd rather go somewhere else, feel free to scan this guide and check out the information on the four world card options. Keep in mind that as you venture up to the top of the castle, the monsters get more difficult to defeat.

The second floor is remarkably small in comparison to the first floor, especially when you consider that one of the regular rooms on the map is the Key to Rewards room, while another room is set aside as the exit room. This leaves four regular rooms to explore as you complete the quest in the story rooms. If you have a difficult time with the boss(es) for a world you've chosen, don't forget that you can reopen the regular rooms with new cards, giving you plenty of Heartless to fight to hone your skills.

WORLD OPTIONS, SECOND FLOOR

 Agrabah

 Olympus Coliseum

 Wonderland

 Monstro

 Halloween Town

COMMON MAP CARDS

 Strong Initiative

 Lasting Daze

 Calm Bounty

 Moogle Room

FEATURED WORLD

Welcome to Agrabah! Here you must help Aladdin defeat the evil Jafar and win the heart of the princess, Jasmine. Along the way you must defeat hordes of scimitar-wielding Bandits and other Heartless, while gaining experience and picking up new, useful cards. The streets of Agrabah are narrow and winding, but with Aladdin, Goofy and Donald on your side, things shouldn't be too difficult.

WORLD MAP

SECOND FLOOR

AGRABAH

Who is that...?

So, uh, why are you going to the palace, Aladdin?

To the first floor

MAP INFORMATION!

This is a sample map of Agrabah that was created using all *Sorcerous Waking* cards. While the rooms you create probably won't look the same as the ones here, the special door requirements and the layout of the floorplan are identical.

What's this?
Has Aladdin given up on his precious Jasmine already?

Barrel Stand	Barrel	Fruits	Hard Barrel	Large Barrels	Pot Stand	Rugs	Stakes

To the third floor

NEW MAP CARDS

 Tranquil Darkness

 Teeming Darkness

 Feeble Darkness

 Sleeping Darkness

 Premium Room

 White Room

 Black Room

 Martial Waking

 Sorcerous Waking

 Alchemic Waking

 Meeting Ground

 Stagnant Space

 Strong Initiative

 Lasting Daze

 Calm Bounty

 Moment's Reprieve

 Moogle Room

NEW BATTLE CARDS

 Three Wishes

 Ether

 Genie

 Gravity

COMMON HEARTLESS

 Air Soldier

 Bandit

 Barrel Spider

 Fat Bandit

 Green Requiem

 Jafar (boss)

 Shadow

Yellow Opera

NEW SLEIGHTS

Blazing Donald	Sandstorm
Gravira	Showtime
Graviga	

SPECIAL TREASURES IN AGRABAH

When you get your first Calm Bounty card, use it to open a room and you'll get the Gravity magic card. Later on, head back here with a Key to Rewards and use it to open the Key to Rewards room to learn the sleight, Blazing Donald.

CONSERVING MAP CARDS

There may come a time when you want to conserve map cards. Here's a little advice to help you out. Story rooms with more than one door take you in through one and let you leave via another. So, if you want to save a map card, open only one of the rooms adjacent to that story room. After viewing the cut-scene or fighting the boss, the game automatically takes you out one of the other doors, opening that room for free! Rooms opened in this manner resemble rooms created by Tranquil Darkness cards.

Enter the story room from the west door to exit from the south, regardless of whether you've opened the room or not.

NEW MAP CARDS!

As noted in the list of new cards for Agrabah, there are a bunch of new map cards to acquire and use. These cards create new types of rooms with even more helpful conditions. Use the Waking cards to beef up your deck in battle. Sorcerous Waking cards increase the magic cards in your deck by 2 points. Martial Waking does the same to your attack cards, while Alchemic Waking improves your item cards. The other new green cards create rooms in which the Heartless move slowly, or remain stunned longer when you instigate a battle. Finally, the two new blue cards should make things a bit easier. Use the Moogle Room card to open up a Moogle Shop where you can buy and sell cards. Calm Bounty is a must for each floor, as it creates a room with a special treasure chest. Inside you'll find new cards or a sleight.

Agrabah's story is pretty straightforward, making it an excellent choice for the first world after Traverse Town. If you've seen the movie *Aladdin* or played the original *Kingdom Hearts* game, then it shouldn't come as a surprise when you have to help Aladdin take on the evil Jafar in the third story room. However, before you fight the boss, spend some time leveling up and adding to your card deck!

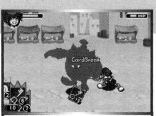

The Fat Bandit is just one of a family of Heartless that are invulnerable to frontal attacks. To counteract their defenses, dodge behind them and slash them in the back!

Taking on Barrel Spiders is a good way to level up once you've defeated all the Heartless on a floor.

AGRABAH'S SPECIAL TREASURE SPOT

Agrabah rooms feature a special Treasure Spot that doesn't appear very frequently. While exploring the town, look for a wooden awning comprised of three poles that overhangs any upper

level window. If you jump down and land on one of them, you'll get a surprise: namely treasure! However, you can only jump *down* to this Treasure Spot; Sora's too short to jump on top of it.

Agrabah is full of new Heartless that are unique to Agrabah. The Bandit wields a large scimitar and has a much longer reach than the standard Shadow. The Fat Bandit is a type of Heartless that you'll see over and over again in the game. Because of its large belly, it doesn't take damage from the front. To inflict damage, Dodge Roll past this creature and get a few attacks in on its backside before it turns around. Blizzard-based attacks also work well on this portly foe.

Also, watch out for Barrel Spiders masquerading as harmless, treasure-spewing barrels. If you smack one with Sora's Keyblade, it comes to life and attacks! These monsters are fierce competitors, preferring to blow themselves up rather than face defeat.

While exploring the area, be on the lookout for the **Three Wishes** Keyblade. Agrabah is the home of this new attack card. Note that after you've obtained your first Three Wishes card, you can pick up more at Moogle Shops anywhere in the game. If you don't want to spend any money on the cards, look for more in the Treasure Spots of Agrabah.

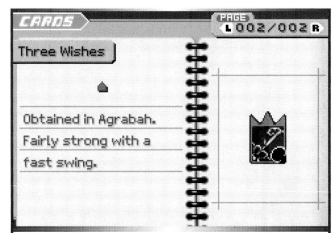

CARDS	PAGE L 002/002 R

Three Wishes

Obtained in Agrabah. Fairly strong with a fast swing.

After acquiring a new card, whether it's from a treasure chest, Treasure Spot or enemy, you can find them almost anywhere you go. The only exceptions are the Keyblades that are unique to a specific world, like the Three Wishes card. If you want more, search the Treasure Spots in that world or purchase them from a Moogle Shop.

Naturally, Aladdin joins the party as a third friend (along with Goofy and Donald) in Agrabah. When you summon him with one of the Aladdin cards that pop up in battle, he shadows Sora while he runs around the battlefield, swinging his sword at the enemy.

Explore Agrabah to its fullest, then head for the story rooms. Watch out for a small battle at the end of the Key of Guidance cut-scene. Win this fight to acquire your first precious **Ether card**. Ether works like the Potion card except that it recycles magic cards instead of attack cards. If you create a deck filled mostly with magic cards, then replace the Potion card with an Ether card.

ALADDIN

A young man who lives in Agrabah and dreams of meeting Princess Jasmine. Aladdin became Genie's master when he found the magic lamp. At first Aladdin wanted to become a prince and impress Jasmine, but in the end he gave Genie his freedom and decided to show Jasmine his true self.

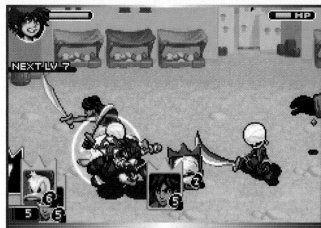

Aladdin can be a great asset in battle, especially when fighting a field full of Fat Bandits!

The Ether card is a welcome addition to decks made up mostly of magic cards. To get one, simply defend Jasmine from the Heartless!

BOSS BATTLE JAFAR

Don't worry about falling into the lava, since you can't! Use the moving levels to stay out of harm's way.

Jafar is NOT the target in this battle! No attack, whether it's physical or magical, will do any damage! Instead, look for Iago flying overhead and defeat him to shrink Jafar back down to size.

The final story room in Agrabah pits you against Jafar. Not only has he turned into a flaming red giant Genie, but he's also turned the area into a burning lava pit. You are forced to combat him on a small rectangle of land, which consists of three elevating platforms. This battle looks tough until you know the secret to success!

Jafar isn't the real target in this battle; he's powerful enough to guard against any attacks. Your true foe is the sharp-tongued parrot, Iago, who flies overhead holding the magic lamp in his beak. Defeat Iago to recover the lamp and Jafar loses all his power!

DECK STRATEGIES

Defeating Jafar doesn't require much beyond a default deck of cards. If you want to change things around, do the following: Take out any magic cards and replace them with attack cards. This lone foe's mode of transportation is such that you can't successfully aim a simple Blizzard attack. Simba, which is a must against groups of enemies, isn't really necessary against single enemy battles like this. Retain your Cure and Potion cards since they'll come in handy in the heat of battle. If you have space remaining, add the Guard Armor enemy card to your deck to give your attacks extra distance.

JAFAR

  IAGO

A sorcerer and Agrabah's royal vizier. Jafar stole the magic lamp from Aladdin and, with Genie's power, schemed to become ruler of Agrabah.

A cunning and chatty parrot. Iago flies about Agrabah, serving as the evil Jafar's eyes and ears.

BOSS BATTLE JAFAR

However, reaching Iago isn't all that easy but the rising platforms help to get within fighting range. First, select the Guard Armor card from your enemy cards and activate it, then start jumping and targeting Iago with Sora's Keyblade when you get high enough to reach him. Sora floats in mid-air when you can get a triple-hit combo. When the trick card appears during the battle, use it to raise all three of the platforms to their highest level, making it easier to get at Iago.

Don't forget about Iago's master, Jafar. His main job is to distract and damage Sora with his three main attacks. Watch out for laser beams, giant lava boulders, and a mean "pound the ground" attack. You can avoid all of Jafar's attacks by dodging them or card breaking, or you can hide behind (or in-between) the raised platforms.

Once you defeat Iago, you receive the **Jafar card** and, after a cut-scene, the **Genie card**.

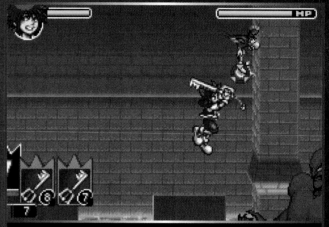

You can reach Iago with attack cards when the platforms are at their middle or highest level. Try to attack him with three consecutive hits at a time.

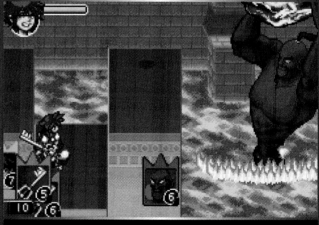

Use the moving platforms to your advantage by putting them between you and Jafar's attacks!

GENIE

All-powerful but captive of the magic lamp, Genie must grant the lamp's holder three wishes. He longs for freedom but can only get it if someone uses a wish to set him free.

Fortunately, nothing much happens in the hallway on the way from the second floor to the third floor. Sora and his pals try to determine how the castle is affecting their memories and an enigmatic character is introduced. Time to move on to the challenges of the third floor!

CASTLE OBLIVION, THIRD FLOOR

The third floor's floorplan provides a little more room to play around in. With 10 rooms, you'll have an opportunity to try out more types of map cards and defeat more Heartless. For this floor, the default choice of Olympus Coliseum was used. The size of the floor makes it a good choice for worlds like this that feature two boss battles. Keep this in mind when you choose a world to recreate on this floor.

WORLD OPTIONS, THIRD FLOOR

 Agrabah

 Olympus Coliseum

 Wonderland

 Monstro

 Halloween Town

COMMON MAP CARDS

 Strong Initiative

 Lasting Daze

 Calm Bounty

 Moogle Room

FEATURED WORLD

In Olympus Coliseum, Sora and his pals find themselves involved in a contest to battle the champion Hercules. Their competitor is none other than that spiky-haired hero from *Final Fantasy VII*, Cloud! The goals in this world are to prevent Cloud from winning the contest and Hades from taking his revenge against the noble Hercules.

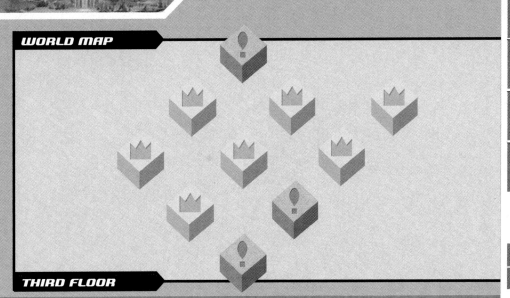

WORLD MAP

THIRD FLOOR

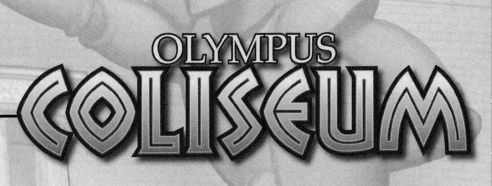

OLYMPUS COLISEUM

OLYMPUS COLISEUM

To the second floor

| Barrel Trio | Barrel | Column | Large Block | Stone Block |

MAP INFORMATION!

This is a sample map of Olympus Coliseum that was created using all *Sleeping Darkness cards*. While the rooms you create won't look the same as the ones here, the special door requirements and the layout of the floorplan are identical.

SPECIAL TREASURES IN OLYMPUS COLISEUM

First things first: When you open a Calm Bounty room in the Coliseum, you learn the helpful sleight **Blizzard Raid**.

Next, when you return to Olympus Coliseum with a Key to Rewards card, you can open the hidden room to get the **Metal Chocobo** attack card.

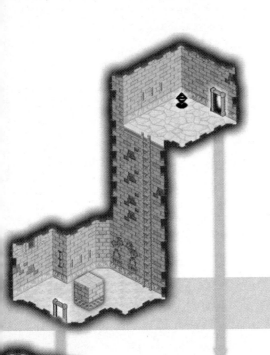

To the fourth floor

NEW BATTLE CARDS

 Olympia

 Cloud

 Hi-Potion

 Metal Chocobo

COMMON HEARTLESS

 Barrel Spider

 Blue Rhapsody

 Bouncywild

 Cloud (boss)

 Hades (boss)

 Large Body

 Powerwild

 Shadow

MAP CARDS

 Tranquil Darkness

 Teeming Darkness

 Feeble Darkness

 Sleeping Darkness

 Premium Room

 White Room

 Black Room

 Martial Waking

 Sorcerous Waking

 Alchemic Waking

 Meeting Ground

 Stagnant Space

 Strong Initiative

 Lasting Daze

Calm Bounty

Moment's Reprieve

Moogle Room

NEW SLEIGHTS

Blizzard Raid

Cross-slash

Omnislash

PREMIUM CARDS

Every once and a while—if you are lucky!— a small black and gold premium prize (marked "P") will appear along with experience prizes after defeating a Heartless. Pick it up, as this prize opens up a Premium Bonus at the end of the battle. This enables you to upgrade a card to a coveted premium card. Premium cards have their pros and cons, though.

To increase your chance of getting a premium prize, open a room using the Premium Room map card. You are almost guaranteed to find at least one during your battles there.

On the plus side, they cost less CP to use which comes in handy if you turn an upper level card into a premium card. The down side is that you can only use this card once in battle; it doesn't reload like a normal card.

At the end of a successful battle, you can win either a map card or an enemy card. Enemy cards are rare treasures, but necessary if you are a defensive player. To increase your chance of getting an enemy card, create rooms using the Teeming Darkness map card. And remember, you can only win the enemy card of the last Heartless you kill in a battle. If you are trying to get a specific one, plot the ending of your battles accordingly!

Olympus Coliseum is like any other classically themed environment. Columns line the streets and friezes of flexing gladiators decorate the walls. Watch out for Barrel Spiders hiding amongst the barrels!

The Heartless in Olympus Coliseum consist of familiar faces and new foes. The Blue Rhapsody appears again and a new common enemy is introduced, the Large Body. Large Body troops are similar to the Fat Bandits in Agrabah in that they have

Watch out for the banana peels that litter the floor when fighting the Powerwilds and Bouncywilds! Trip on one and Sora will fall flat on his back, or at least get mildly stunned.

highly protected fronts. Attack from the rear to take them down. In addition to the "normal" troops, expect to encounter the monkey-like Bouncywilds and Powerwilds. These creatures are tough and the Bouncywilds throw banana peels in addition to their standard bullets.

Unlike other worlds, no companion joins your party of friends while in Olympus Coliseum. However, you'll have Simba and Genie cards (if you completed Agrabah) if you choose to stock them. Sometimes using a summon magic card is just as good as calling upon your friends.

Donald and Goofy are the only friends you can actually summon while fighting through Olympus Coliseum, but stocking the Genie magic card is almost as good!

KEYBLADE HUNTING IN OLYMPUS

Olympus Coliseum has its own special Keyblade too! It's called the *Olympia* and it is hidden inside one of the Treasure Spots scattered around the world. Remember, it shows up randomly, so trigger the Treasure Spots until it pops up. You might also find it in the Moogle Shop if you've opened a Moogle Room.

BOSS BATTLE CLOUD

Adding to the danger of this battle is the attack range of Cloud's sword in comparison to Sora's. Watch out for Cloud's special attacks, since they can connect from across the field.

The silver lining to this battle is that one day all of Cloud's powerful attacks will be yours to command. Of course, you have to defeat him (and later Hades), first!

Cloud is a tough opponent at this point. He has a lot of high-numbered cards in his deck and can pull off some pretty powerful combos. Success comes from Sora's ability to dodge Cloud's attacks while still landing his attacks. At this point, you should know several sleights. Use them! Sleights and basic combo attacks are tough to card break because their values are based upon the sum of the cards involved. This enables you to use lower-numbered cards safely and effectively, making it less likely that your opponent will card break them.

Cloud tends to attack in combos, too, which makes it harder to card break his attacks if you attack with single cards. Since his special attacks, like Omnislash, are especially harmful and difficult to dodge, keep your fingers on the L and R Buttons to create your own combos to defeat him.

Defeat Cloud to receive a Hi-Potion card. And, having survived his wrath, you can look forward to the end of this world, when you get the Cloud magic card to add to your deck. Just think of the damage you can cause when you stock two or three Cloud cards in your deck!

INSIDE THE BOSS'S DECK

Cloud has three types of attacks and two sleights. The "A" and "B" attack cards cause Cloud to perform different slash attacks. When Cloud uses either an "A" or "B" card while he's in the air, he performs a jump and slash attack. Cloud's sleight Cross-slash occurs when Cloud stocks 3 "B" cards. Omnislash appears when Cloud combines a "B" card + "A" card + "B" card.

Cloud's deck is comprised of the following cards:

"A" attack cards: 0 (x1); 1 (x1); 2 (x2); 3 (x2); 4 (x2); 5 (x1); 6 (x1); 7 (x1); 8 (x1)

"B" attack cards: 0 (x1); 1 (x1); 2 (x2); 3 (x2); 4 (x2); 5 (x1); 6 (x1); 7 (x1); 8 (x1)

Hi-Potion: 7 (x1)

DECK STRATEGIES

Again, at this point in the game, unless you've invested a lot of time and Moogle Points at the Moogle Shops, your deck is likely to be very similar to the one you started the game with. Ultimately, you should start replacing low numbered cards with cards in the 8-9 or zero range. These high numbered cards enable you to card break the enemy's attacks more efficiently and make your own attacks less likely to be cardbroken.

BOSS BATTLE HADES

This is a difficult fight. It's not that Hades is particularly fast or that his deck is full of tough to break cards. Hades has the power of fire and there are times when you can't escape his burning hands.

Hades has two special sleights, Temper Flare and Firaga Ball. When using Temper Flare, he flicks flames with enough force to send Sora flying across the room. Firaga Ball is easy to dodge as long as you stay next to Hades. However, this is a tough proposition, especially as you get closer to defeating him. Hades is fond of lighting up his hands and drenching Sora in a stream of fire. If you can't card break this attack, get out of its path. This is where you'll sustain most of your damage.

To defeat Hades, you must disrupt his attacks. To do this, fight in combos or acquire high-numbered attack cards. You must also heal when necessary. Stock a couple of Cure cards and use them in combination to get the most healing. It is also a good idea to time your healing with Hades's recharge breaks.

Once defeated, Hades yields the **Hades card**. Before you leave the final story room, you also receive the **Cloud card**.

DECK STRATEGIES

For this battle, spend some time getting a Moogle Room card and opening a Moogle Shop. Hades is a tough boss to defeat, so make sure your deck has cards in the mid to high-number range (6-zero) to card break his fiery attacks. Also, stock at least two Cure cards to take care of the damage that he causes.

Hades throws his Firaga Ball one way, while Sora runs in the opposite direction. This attack is easy to dodge if you are near Hades when it starts, as you can determine which direction the attack is going.

The blue card indicates that Hades's hands are about to erupt in flame.

The halfway point is when the battle gets really rough. Keep an eye on Sora's health gauge and look for opportunities to unload on Hades!

INSIDE THE BOSS'S DECK

Hades has three attacks and two sleights. The first, a flamethrower, is triggered by his blue "A" attack card. His second attack, a fire shot, is triggered when he uses a red "B" attack card. His final normal attack, a fiery claw, happens when he uses either an "A" or "B" card, while he's colored red from his Temper Flare attack. And speaking of Hades' first sleight, Temper Flare is caused by combining three "A" cards. His second, Firagaball, occurs when he stocks a "B" card + "A" card "B" card while he's red.

Hades' deck is as follows:
"A" attack cards: 0 (x1); 1 (x1); 2 (x1); 3 (x2); 4 (x2); 5 (x2); 6 (x2); 7 (x1); 8 (x1)
"B" attack cards: 1 (x1); 2 (x1); 3 (x2); 4 (x2); 5 (x2); 6 (x2); 7 (x1); 8 (x1), 9 (x1)
Elixir: 0 (x1); 4 (x1)
Hades and Red Nocturne enemy cards

CLOUD

A swordsman hired by Hades to take out Hercules. Cloud seeks the true memories he has lost. Were they memories of someone dear to him, or memories of his own hazy past?

HERCULES

Son of the gods Zeus and Hera, but not a god himself. With godlike strength and a gentle heart, Hercules is a true hero. He has never lost at the Coliseum games.

INTO THE CASTLE HALLS, BETWEEN THE THIRD AND FOURTH FLOOR

Once again, the hallway between the floors is quiet as Sora and his friends check the state of their memories and the Organization plots in the depths of the castle.

CASTLE OBLIVION, FOURTH FLOOR

The fourth floor grows by a room and has bigger door requirements. Otherwise, the differences between this floor and the others you've explored are minimal.

This walkthrough follows the default world, Wonderland. Wonderland's story is similar to Agrabah in that you have a minor battle to win in one of the story rooms before you can take on the main boss in the final Key to Truth room. Unlike Olympus Coliseum, not much deck development is required to clear this world, making it a pleasant place to visit and level up before undertaking the challenges of Monstro and Halloween Town.

WORLD OPTIONS, FOURTH FLOOR

 Agrabah

 Olympus Coliseum

 Wonderland

 Monstro

Halloween Town

COMMON MAP CARDS

 Strong Initiative

 Lasting Daze

 Calm Bounty

 Moogle Room

FEATURED WORLD

All is not right in the world of Wonderland! The Queen is in a rage because someone has been stealing her memories! The natural culprit—in her mind, anyway—is Alice. Defend Alice and protect the kingdom from the memory thief!

WORLD MAP

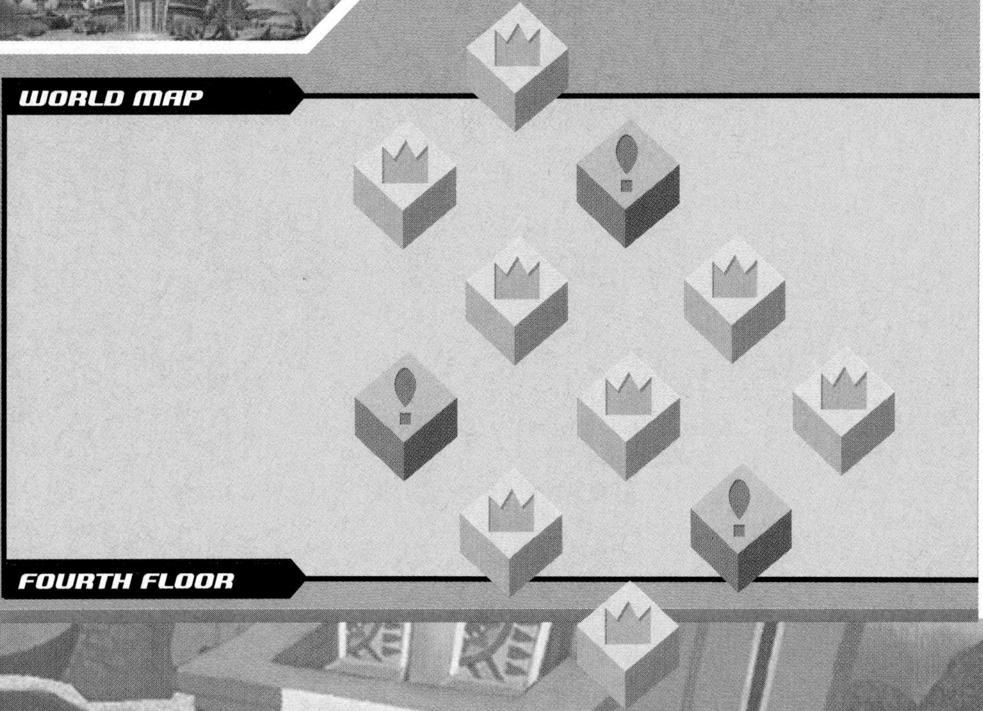

FOURTH FLOOR

WONDER LAND

WELCOME TO CASTLE OBLIVION

CHARACTERS

GAME BASICS

CASTLE OBLIVION

FIRST FLOOR
SECOND FLOOR
THIRD FLOOR
FOURTH FLOOR
FIFTH FLOOR
SIXTH FLOOR
SEVENTH FLOOR
EIGHTH FLOOR
NINTH FLOOR
TENTH FLOOR
ELEVENTH FLOOR
TWELFTH FLOOR
THIRTEENTH FLOOR

SECRETS OF THE GAME

THE CARDS

BESTIARY

WONDERLAND

NEW BATTLE CARDS

 Lady Luck

 Stop

COMMON HEARTLESS

 Card Soldier (boss)

 Creeper Plant

 Crescendo

 Large Body

 Red Nocturne

 Shadow

 Soldier

 Trickmaster (boss)

NEW SLEIGHTS

Stopra

Stopga

Stop Raid

MAP CARDS

 Tranquil Darkness

 Teeming Darkness

 Feeble Darkness

 Sleeping Darkness

 Premium Room

 White Room

 Black Room

 Martial Waking

 Sorcerous Waking

 Alchemic Waking

 Meeting Ground

 Stagnant Space

 Strong Initiative

 Lasting Daze

 Calm Bounty

Moment's Reprieve

Moogle Room

Alice! Do you understand the charges against you?

SPECIAL TREASURES IN WONDERLAND

Look for the magic card Stop in a treasure chest in your first Calm Bounty room. Later, return with a Key to Rewards card to get the coordinating *Stop Raid* sleight.

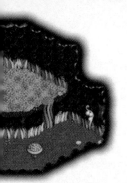

To the fifth floor

WELCOME TO
CASTLE OBLIVION

CHARACTERS

GAME BASICS

CASTLE
OBLIVION

FIRST FLOOR

SECOND FLOOR

THIRD FLOOR

FOURTH FLOOR

FIFTH FLOOR

SIXTH FLOOR

SEVENTH FLOOR

EIGHTH FLOOR

NINTH FLOOR

TENTH FLOOR

ELEVENTH FLOOR

TWELFTH FLOOR

THIRTEENTH FLOOR

SECRETS OF THE
GAME

THE CARDS

BESTIARY

MAP INFORMATION!

This is a sample map of Wonderland that was created using all *Meeting Ground* cards. While the rooms you create won't look the same as the ones here, the special door requirements and the layout of the floorplan are identical.

Gawrsh, what's with the sudden change of scenery?

Is that right?
Well, you saved me all the same.

To the third floor

| Big Tree | Large Yellow Mushroom | Red Flower | Yellow Mushroom |

MOOGLE ROOMS

By now you should have acquired a Moogle Room map card at the end of a battle. When you use these cards to open a door, a Moogle Shop appears. Moogle Shops are places where you can buy new cards and/or sell off old ones. You can open as many shops as you like on a floor, but it's a good idea to buy the moogles out of card packs before you leave.

Moogles sell packs of five cards. You can buy sets of attack cards, magic cards, item cards, or packs that contains a mix from all three categories. When you visit a newly-opened Moogle Shop, you receive a free pack of cards. To buy more, sell off your old, unwanted cards or gather lots of the Moogle Point drops from the Treasure Spots.

Since the price of card packs is fairly cheap at this stage of the game, it's a good idea to get as many high numbered cards in your deck as possible. The prices go up (way up!) once you hit the seventh floor!

WONDERLAND'S SPECIAL TREASURE SPOT

Wonderland has an unusual and rare Treasure Spot that only appears when you open large rooms with cards like Teeming Darkness. The giant tree cannot be triggered with a flick of Sora's Keyblade and it's too tall for Sora to jump on top. Instead, find a platform high enough to jump over to the top of the tree. Act quickly upon triggering the prizes, because they come out from the bottom of the tree!

ALICE

A curious girl who fell down the rabbit hole into Wonderland. Alice was falsely accused of stealing the Queen of Hearts's memory and put on trial, but we intervened and helped her clear her name.

THE QUEEN OF HEARTS

A selfish ruler who commands an army of card soldiers. A Heartless stole the Queen's memory, but she accused Alice and put her on trial.

Wonderland is like a big garden, so it should come as no surprise that the new monsters you encounter here are flower-themed. The Crescendos flit about and are rather tough. The Creeper Plants have long roots that can trip up Sora, plus they can spit seeds if you get too close. In battle, take out the Creeper Plants first, then concentrate on the rest of the Heartless.

As you open and explore the rooms of Wonderland, make sure you trigger all Treasure Spots until you get the **Lady Luck card**. This is Wonderland's unique Keyblade; you'll want to find at least one before moving on to the next level.

The Creeper Plant has two means of attack: its roots and its seeds. They may be stationary monsters, but their reach is longer than you may expect.

The number of flowers scattered around Wonderland makes it easy to find the Lady Luck attack card.

BOSS BATTLE CARD SOLDIERS

The Card Soldiers battle is on the same difficulty level as any of the generic Heartless battles you've fought on the way to the Key of Beginnings room. Prepare to face two waves of soldiers. They'll try to gang up on Sora but they don't have any powerful combo attacks, so fight them off in normal fashion.

This battle isn't that difficult. Using the Simba card enables you to inflict damage on the entire group, provided they're standing in front of Simba when he roars.

DECK STRATEGIES

Now is the time to start thinking about strategies for defeating groups of enemies. One of the better approaches is the Simba deck, which revolves around the use of the Simba card. At this point, you probably only have a few of these cards in your inventory (unless you've visited the Moogle Shops) but that's a start. The concept here is to place three or more Simba cards at the start of your deck and use them to inflict damage on the enemies in front of Sora. Three Simba cards in a row (*not in a combo*) should inflict enough damage to take out the first wave of enemies. If it doesn't do the trick, finish them with a stroke of Sora's Keyblade. As the game progresses and you pick up more cards and learn more sleights, combine the power of the Simba card and its basic sleight, Proud Roar, with other long-range sleights to create even more mayhem.

BOSS BATTLE TRICKMASTER

The Trickmaster relies on two basic attacks. For one attack, he crosses his flaming sticks and shoots a fireball. The second attack has him slamming the sticks down on the floor causing a minor shockwave. It's possible to dodge or card break both attacks.

The simple way to defeat the Trickmaster is to pin him in a corner and attack him with Sora's Keyblade. When the Trickmaster bends over, hit his vulnerable spot.

Additionally, you can defeat the Trickmaster by using the trick card. This plops a dinette set in the middle of the battlefield, pinning the Trickmaster in place and providing a higher perch from which to attack.

DECK STRATEGIES

Since there is only one enemy in this battle, take out any Simba cards (if there are any in your deck) and replace them with high-numbered attack cards. Since the Trickmaster uses fire in his attacks, consider adding more Cure cards or stock the ones you have when using them in battle.

The Trickmaster is an interesting boss. This memory thief is little more than a spindly circus performer who attacks with flaming juggling sticks. You cannot extinguish the fire, but you can easily card break the Trickmaster's two basic attacks. This boss's gangly limbs prevent him from mounting consecutive attacks or even attacking on a frequent basis.

Ultimately, this battle is easy to win as long as you have a decent deck. If you've been purchasing cards from the Moogle Shops, most of your attack cards should be at level 7 or higher. This should enable you to break almost any attack the Trickmaster mounts while defending your attacks from his cards. If you get too close to his flaming sticks and take too much damage, step back and heal before diving back into the fray. Defeating the Trickmaster nets you the *Trickmaster enemy card*.

INTO THE CASTLE HALLS, BETWEEN THE FOURTH AND FIFTH FLOORS

Once again, the action between floors is non-existent. Don't get used to it! Things are going to start heating up very soon...

CASTLE OBLIVION, FIFTH FLOOR

The fifth floor is made up of 12 rooms and, if you choose the default World, Monstro, as is the case here, you'll need all of that space to get your deck in order for the final challenge in the Key to Truth room! On this floor, the three story rooms are spread out on the edges, which means it will take a lot of work hard to reach their entrances. Use the time wisely to level up Sora and build your deck.

WORLD OPTIONS, FIFTH FLOOR

 Agrabah

 Olympus Coliseum

 Wonderland

 Monstro

 Halloween Town

COMMON MAP CARDS

 Strong Initiative

 Lasting Daze

 Calm Bounty

 Moogle Room

FEATURED WORLD

In Monstro, Sora's traveling mate Jiminy Cricket is reunited with his old pals Pinocchio and Geppetto. These beloved characters join in a fight to leave the belly of the whale. However, just defeating the boss isn't enough to secure the party's release. You'll need to defeat wave after wave of Heartless before Monstro blows its top!

MONSTRO

MONSTRO

SPECIAL TREASURES IN MONSTRO

Both of the special treasures found in Monstro are sleights. From the first Calm Bounty room, you'll take away **Fire Raid**, while from the Key to Rewards room you'll learn the **Aqua Splash** sleight.

MAP INFORMATION!

This sample map of Monstro was created using all *Sleeping Darkness cards*. While the rooms you create probably won't look the same as the ones here, the special door requirements and the layout of the floorplan are identical.

To the fourth floor

Barrel	Big Blue Thing	Big Pink Thing	Small Blue Thing

You know Geppetto worries when you wander off by yourself.

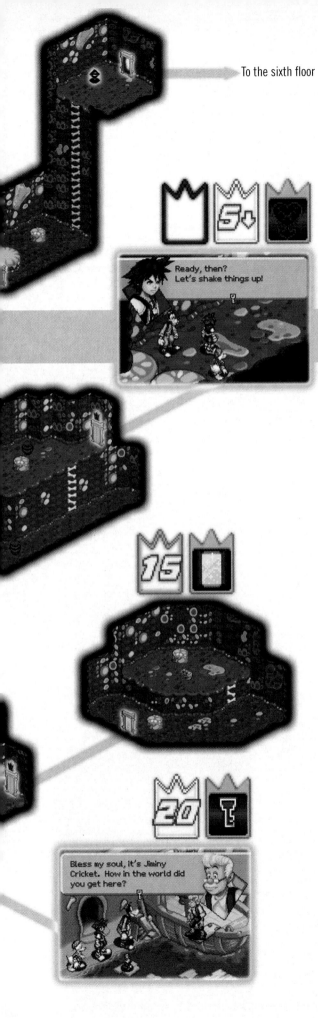

To the sixth floor

To the sixth floor

Ready, then? Let's shake things up!

Bless my soul, it's Jiminy Cricket. How in the world did you get here?

LARGE ROOMS VS SMALL ROOMS

You've should know by now how the different map cards work. Some create normal sized rooms, while others create rooms that are unusually small or unusually large. While it may seem easier to create only small rooms, keep the following in mind. The size of the room largely dictates the number and type of Treasure Spots that appear. If you are trying to collect Moogle Points to buy lots of card packs at a Moogle Shop, you'll want rooms with lots of different Treasure Spots. Consider placing Moogle Rooms near larger rooms made with cards like Teeming Darkness and Strong Initiative. By following this technique, you won't have to run too far away to get the precious Moogle Point prizes needed to buy those cards!

NEW BATTLE CARDS

 Wishing Star

 Dumbo

COMMON HEARTLESS

Air Soldier

Barrel Spider

Green Requiem

Large Body

Parasite Cage (boss)

Search Ghost

Shadow

Tornado Step

Yellow Opera

NEW SLEIGHTS

Fire Raid

Aqua Splash

Splash

MAP CARDS

 Tranquil Darkness

 Teeming Darkness

Feeble Darkness

Sleeping Darkness

Premium Room

 White Room

 Black Room

 Martial Waking

 Sorcerous Waking

 Alchemic Waking

 Meeting Ground

 Stagnant Space

Strong Initiative

Lasting Daze

Calm Bounty

Moment's Reprieve

 Moogle Room

This world takes place within the belly of the giant whale Monstro. The Treasure Spots here resemble jello molds and pink membranes, but the Heartless are all creatures you meet on land. The new Heartless include the swift and acrobatic Tornado Steps and the spooky Search Ghosts. The Search Ghosts have the ability to warp around the battlefield, putting them out of reach when you want to attack and popping up from behind when you want to escape.

Entire herds of Tornado Steps can spell trouble. Take them out using cards that have large fields of effect, like the Simba card. However, don't be surprised if the Tornado Steps get out of the way before the attack can connect.

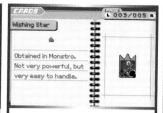

As you fight to the story rooms, keep hitting and jumping on the world's Treasure Spots until you get the Wishing Star attack card, which is Monstro's unique Keyblade.

PINOCCHIO

A wooden puppet Geppetto made, brought to life by the Blue Fairy. To become a real boy, Pinocchio has to learn bravery, kindness, and honesty. He and Geppetto were swallowed by Monstro, but they escaped with a little help from us.

BOSS BATTLE PARASITE CAGE

The main boss for this world appears in the Key of Guidance room as you look for Pinocchio. Unfortunately, you arrive a bit too late. To free Pinocchio, you must defeat the Parasite Cage.

The Parasite Cage sits on a small platform in the middle of a pool of green stomach acid. You have two choices: You can fight from the four islands circling in front of the monster with magic (or other wide-range attacks), or you can dive into the acid to confront the boss head on. Note, however, that hopping into the acid does cause damage and it takes Sora a few moments to recover. If you get a trick card during the battle, use it to provide protection for Sora from the acid for a short while. This can provide time to get up close and personal with the Parasite Cage.

If you walk in the acid for too long, Sora will take damage.

When you use the trick card, a thin membrane protects Sora from the acid's burn for a short period of time.

DECK STRATEGIES

The Parasite Cage requires a deck that has mid- to high-level cards. If you are comfortable with using magic and have enough cards in your deck, cast spell combos on this boss. If you prefer melee battle, then stock your deck with attack cards. Of course, two or three Cure cards are a must and perhaps a Potion or Ether.

The Parasite Cage's spit attack is gross and deadly!

The body slam attack comes into play about halfway across the battlefield from the Parasite Cage. Watch for it if you are trying to heal or cast spells from that point.

As long as you are successfully attacking the Parasite Cage, you are safe from the effects of the acid. However, if you get card broken or hit with an attack, expect to be knocked back into the drink!

The acid isn't the only danger that Sora faces—the Parasite Cage is pretty fierce, too. Watch out for this boss's spit attack. It can hit Sora from most anywhere on the wheel of islands, knocking him off the platform and inflicting damage. Get too close and the Parasite Cage slams its arms down in the acid, causing a shockwave of damage. The Parasite Cage also has a nice body slam attack that can—and will—take you by surprise!

The best way to defeat the Parasite Cage is to throw caution to the wind and rush the boss's platform. If your cards are a high enough level, you can keep up a stream of consecutive attacks and the Parasite Cage won't be able to put a stop to the attack. If Sora's HP gauge reaches critical levels, back off and heal with a Cura or Curaga.

BOSS BATTLE
THE HEARTLESS CHALLENGE

The battle with the Parasite Cage gives Sora and his pals an escape plan. They figure that if they defeat enough of the Heartless in Monstro's belly fast enough, he'll spit them out. This is the challenge: Defeat waves of Heartless in bulk and do it as quickly as possible!

The Simba deck enables you to defeat a wave of Shadows in about three cards. So if you have about six in your deck, you can knock out two waves immediately. Regardless of your approach in this battle, the idea is to fill the gauge before the Heartless run out. If you do this, Monstro spits Sora and his friends out. If you don't, you get the opportunity to heal and take the challenge all over again. For winning the battle, you receive the Dumbo summon card.

The Shadows attack in waves of eight in a circular pattern. This makes it tough to wade in with Sora's Keyblade and attack a group of monsters. Using a Simba card enables you to attack all of them at once.

Once the gauge is full, it's time to finish off the remaining Shadows and go home.

DECK STRATEGIES

In the Wonderland area, the creation of the Simba deck approach was discussed. The suggestions given there apply equally to this battle. To defeat the greatest number of Heartless at once, you need a card or attack that has a large range of effect. The Simba card inflicts damage on any enemy standing or floating in front of Sora. Put as many of these cards at the start of your deck (no card lower than a 6) and use them one at a time. Don't use them in combos because you'll need all of them when you reload your deck. Any unfilled slots should be filled with the cards of your choice to mop up any remaining Heartless.

GEPPETTO

A gentle and earnest clockmaker who carved Pinocchio from a block of wood. Geppetto was swallowed by Monstro, boat and all, while searching for Pinocchio. The two were reunited inside the giant whale and escaped with our help.

WELCOME TO CASTLE OBLIVION

CHARACTERS

GAME BASICS

CASTLE OBLIVION

First Floor

Second Floor

Third Floor

Fourth Floor

Fifth Floor

Sixth Floor

Seventh Floor

Eighth Floor

Ninth Floor

Tenth Floor

Eleventh Floor

Twelfth Floor

Thirteenth Floor

SECRETS OF THE GAME

THE CARDS

BESTIARY

INTO THE CASTLE HALLS, BETWEEN THE FIFTH AND SIXTH FLOORS

Nothing exciting happens in the hallway between floors. However, the end of Larxene and Axel's conversation should key you in to what lies ahead.

CASTLE OBLIVION, SIXTH FLOOR

The sixth floor has 13 rooms and the story rooms quite spread out, meaning it will take some hard work to get them. Not that it should be a problem at this point in the game. For this part of the walkthrough, the default world, Halloween Town, was chosen. Taken straight from Tim Burton's film *The Nightmare Before Christmas*, this world seems the perfect environment for Heartless and features some of the coolest Treasure Spots in the game.

WORLD OPTIONS, SIXTH FLOOR

 Agrabah

 Olympus Coliseum

 Wonderland

 Monstro

 Halloween Town

COMMON BATTLE CARDS

 Thunder

NEW SLEIGHTS

Thundara

Thundaga

FEATURED WORLD

Halloween Town is a dark and gloomy place, filled with tombs, pumpkins and the occasional bat or ghost. The task here is to help good ol' Jack Skellington with an infestation of Heartless taking over Halloween Town. Normally, Jack loves to have monsters in his town but these creatures are actually hurting residents instead of just scaring them, so they've got to go!

COMMON MAP CARDS

 Alchemic Waking

 Stagnant Space

 Strong Initiative

 Lasting Daze

 Calm Bounty

Moogle Room

WORLD MAP

SIXTH FLOOR

HALLOWEEN TOWN

HALLOWEEN TOWN

Allow me to introduce Dr. Finkelstein, the world-famous genius!

To the fifth floor

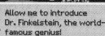

To the fifth floor

SPECIAL TREASURES IN HALLOWEEN TOWN

Once again, sleights reign supreme. In the first Calm Bounty room you open you'll learn the sleight, Gifted Miracle. Later on, return to the Key of Rewards room to learn Gravity Raid.

STRONG INITIATIVE AND LASTING DAZE

If you're feeling a bit overwhelmed by the Heartless in a new world, consider using the green cards Strong Initiative and Lasting Daze. These cards provide an advantage when you instigate a battle in their rooms. When you strike first in Strong Initiative rooms, the first wave of enemies are stunned and they sustain damage equal to about three-quarters of their HP.

Lasting Daze's effect is more subtle. In battles started in these rooms, all waves of Heartless arrive in a stunned state. If you avoid hitting the newly arrived monsters, you can set up sleights and attack combos during this short period of peace.

You fools don't know when to quit! Say...all this running around is making me thirsty!

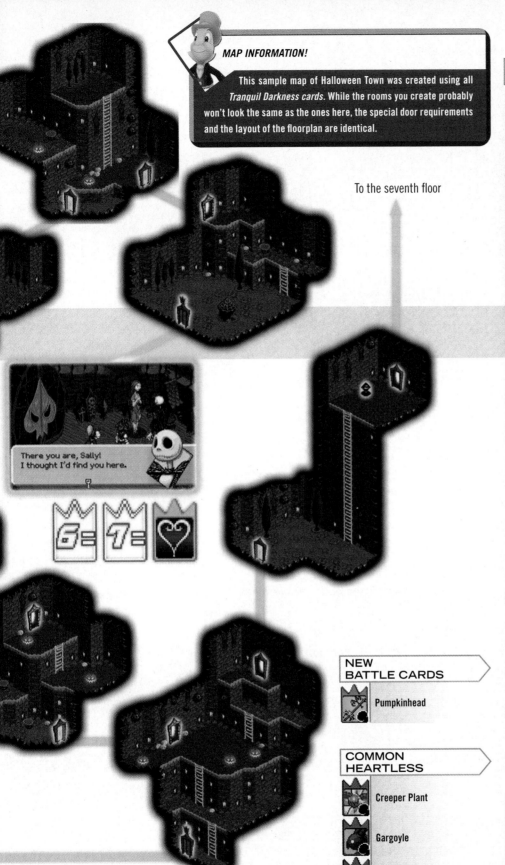

MAP INFORMATION!

This sample map of Halloween Town was created using all *Tranquil Darkness cards*. While the rooms you create probably won't look the same as the ones here, the special door requirements and the layout of the floorplan are identical.

To the seventh floor

There you are, Sally!
I thought I'd find you here.

Hutch | Pumpkin | Tall Tree | Tree Trio EW | Tree Trio NS | Tree Trio RL

MAP CARDS

 Tranquil Darkness

 Teeming Darkness

 Feeble Darkness

 Sleeping Darkness

 Premium Room

 White Room

 Black Room

 Martial Waking

 Sorcerous Waking

 Alchemic Waking

 Meeting Ground

 Stagnant Space

 Strong Initiative

 Lasting Daze

 Calm Bounty

 Moment's Reprieve

 Moogle Room

NEW BATTLE CARDS

 Pumpkinhead

COMMON HEARTLESS

Creeper Plant

Gargoyle

Oogie Boogie (boss)

Search Giant

Wight Knight

NEW SLEIGHTS

Gifted Miracle

Gravity Raid

Surprise!

Terror

HALLOWEEN TOWN'S MANY TREASURE SPOTS

Halloween Town wins the award for the most creative Treasure Spots. Use map cards that create some of the larger rooms to see them all. Watch out for the three trees Treasure Spot. Because Sora can't jump on top of them, you'll need to look for opportunities to drop down on top of them if you want the prizes they contain. Unfortunately, these Treasure Spots appear often but rarely in locations where you can reach them.

While moving through Halloween Town, prepare to run into the Heartless besieging this world. In keeping with the Halloween theme, most of them are the stuff nightmares are made of. The Search Ghost appeared in Monstro, but the Wight Knights and Gargoyles are new to the scene. Gargoyles fly about the battlefield, pelting their opponents with fireballs or attacking them with claws and wings (which attack they use depends on how close Sora is to them). The Wight Knights have long arms that they use in a windmill attack to inflict multiple hits.

Two new opponents, two new attacks. The Gargoyle's fireballs are easily dodged if you see them coming ahead of time. The Wight Knight's windmill attack, however, stuns Sora, leaving him unable to recover in time to escape the rest of the hits.

Halloween Town is one of only two worlds in the first group of world cards that offers a third companion (along with Donald and Goofy) to summon in battle. Agrabah had Aladdin and Halloween Town has Jack Skellington. Jack brings with him two sleights, the standard multi-card attack Surprise!, and the unusual Terror. If you have a couple of summon cards in your deck, use this attack when you get a Jack card in battle.

Stock two summon cards (like Simba) and one Jack card to use Terror, a sleight that unleashes a horde of ghosts on all enemies on the battlefield. This sleight can also be cast outside of Halloween Town using a Simba card, Mushu card, and any item card.

Pumpkinhead

Halloween Town's unique Keyblade is the Pumpkinhead. This attack card has average stats, but it boasts the best recovery and CP cost scores to date. A high recovery stat means that Sora recovers quickly when his attack is card broken.

BOSS BATTLE OOGIE BOOGIE

This is one of the only battles in the game in which the boss attacks using a specific sequence. Oogie Boogie stands on a platform behind a wrought iron fence, protecting him from incoming attacks. Every so often, though, he tosses out three dice. Hitting at least one of them causes the fence to retract by one-third. Destroy the third round of dice and you can jump onto the stage and take Oogie Boogie on face-to-face.

Destroying the dice causes the fence to retract a bit. Once the fence is fully retracted, jump onto the stage and attack Oogie Boogie. Using the trick card immediately lowers the fence, allowing you to attack Oogie Boogie right away.

There is a limited amount of time to attack Oogie Boogie before you are knocked off the stage by an exploding die, which also causes the fence to go back up. However, if you watch Oogie Boogie you can predict where he's going to toss the dice and stay out of the way, thus avoiding damage. Using trick cards when they become available also reduces the chance of taking damage and it enables you to control when you take Oogie on in hand-to-hand combat. This way, you can ensure that you've reloaded your cards and make the most of the time you have to inflict damage on the boss.

DECK STRATEGIES

For this battle, it's best to just go with a simple attack card deck. Stock your deck with your best high-numbered attack cards, a few Cure cards and a Potion or Hi-Potion card.

JACK

Halloween Town's master of the macabre. Jack is always looking for new ways to bring the spooks and shivers of Halloween to all.

OOGIE BOOGIE

A villain who is always plotting against Jack. Oogie Boogie stole Dr. Finkelstein's potion thinking it would make him stronger, but it drove him mad with fear instead.

SALLY

Dr. Finkelstein's helper at the lab. He created her from various odds and ends. Sally is secretly in love with Jack.

DR. FINKELSTEIN

The mad scientist of Halloween Town. He's always immersed in his odd experiments. This time Dr. Finkelstein came up with a potion to restore true memories, only to have it guzzled by Oogie Boogie.

INTO THE CASTLE HALLS, BETWEEN THE SIXTH AND SEVENTH FLOORS

You've run out of world cards, so when you step into the hallway between floors, you can pretty much guarantee that you'll run into one of the members of the mysterious Organization. Larxene is the one you meet on your way to the seventh floor and she's got some interesting things to think about, after you recover from fighting her.

BOSS BATTLE LARXENE

Larxene's specialty is lightning. When she puts together a Lightning Bolt combo, prepare to card break it with a zero card. The rest of the time, prepare to either chase her down to attack her or dodge or card break her "normal" attacks.

The best time to attack Larxene at full force is when she is recharging her attack. If you can pin her in a corner, you can unleash a steady stream of hits.

Defeat Larxene to get your first Thunder card. Larxene also hands over your next set of world cards. Run up to the seventh floor and see what you received!

DECK STRATEGIES

Hopefully, you haven't changed your deck since the Oogie Boogie boss fight. This battle requires that you card break attacks (make sure you have some zero cards on hand), while getting in enough consecutive attacks to harm Larxene.

Thunder magic is what Larxene does best. Watch out for her Lightning Bolt attack, as this sustained attack can leave Sora feeling a bit stunned at the end.

Watch out for Larxene's Thundara attack (blue card) or her lightning bullets (red card). Both attacks are difficult to dodge.

It hardly seems fair to kick Larxene when she's defenseless, but this is your best chance of connecting with multiple hits.

INSIDE THE BOSS'S DECK

Larxene has three different attack cards which trigger three different attacks. The "A" card provokes a combo attack while the "B" card triggers her lethal lightning knives attack. The "C" card is responsible for her deadly Thundara attack. Watch out when she stocks an "A" card + 2 "C" cards, as that signals the approach of her Lightning Bolt sleight.

Her deck is as follows:
"A" attack cards: 0 (x1); 1 (x1); 2 (x1); 3 (x1); 4 (x1); 5 (x1); 6 (x1); 7 (x1); 8 (x1); 9 (x1)
"B" attack cards: 0 (x1); 1 (x1); 2 (x1); 3 (x1); 4 (x1); 5 (x1); 6 (x1); 7 (x1); 8 (x1); 9 (x1)
"C" attack cards: 0 (x1); 1 (x1); 2 (x1); 3 (x1); 4 (x1); 5 (x1); 6 (x1); 7 (x1); 8 (x1); 9 (x1)
Elixir: 2 (x1); 6 (x1)
enemy card: Yellow Opera

WELCOME TO CASTLE OBLIVION

CHARACTERS

GAME BASICS

CASTLE OBLIVION

FIRST FLOOR
SECOND FLOOR
THIRD FLOOR
FOURTH FLOOR
FIFTH FLOOR
SIXTH FLOOR
SEVENTH FLOOR
EIGHTH FLOOR
NINTH FLOOR
TENTH FLOOR
ELEVENTH FLOOR
TWELFTH FLOOR
THIRTEENTH FLOOR

SECRETS OF THE GAME

THE CARDS

BESTIARY

CASTLE OBLIVION, SEVENTH FLOOR

Before you climb the staircase to the seventh floor, Larxene hands over another set of world cards. This time you have four worlds from which to choose over the next four floors. The world cards you receive are **Atlantica** from *The Little Mermaid*, **Hollow Bastion**, **Never Land** from *Peter Pan*, and the **Hundred Acre Wood** from the Winnie the Pooh stories.

As always, it's entirely the player's choice as to which world to visit on each floor. For this section, the walkthrough is structured around the default world for each floor, starting with Atlantica.

WORLD OPTIONS, SEVENTH FLOOR

 Atlantica

 Never Land

 Hollow Bastion

 Hundred Acre Wood

COMMON BATTLE CARDS

 Aero

COMMON BATTLE CARDS

 Almighty Darkness

 Looming Darkness

 White Room

FEATURED WORLD

All is not right in Atlantica. The Princess Ariel is acting strangely and king Triton is missing his trident. Are the two events connected or is it just coincidence? Put your detective skills to work to solve this underwater dilemma.

NEW SLEIGHTS

Aerora

Aeroga

WORLD MAP

SEVENTH FLOOR

ATLANTICA

ATLANTICA

MAP INFORMATION!

This sample map of Atlantica was created using all *Martial Waking cards*. While the rooms you create probably won't look the same as the ones here, the special door requirements and the layout of the floorplan are identical.

Clam   Coral   Large Rock

NEW MAP CARDS!

Eight new map cards join the ranks upon entering the seventh floor. These cards have unusual properties, opening doors with super-powerful Heartless, special Heartless you won't find anywhere else, or enemies guarding great treasures.

The biggest addition to the field of map cards is the *Key to Rewards card*. This card enables you to finally open those hidden rooms on all the floors you've visited thus far. Each world (with the exception of the final one) has one of these special Key to Rewards rooms. Inside you'll find a single treasure chest containing either a special sleight or a rare card. Of course, since this card falls into the same category as the Keycards that open the story rooms, you can only have one at a time. When you get one, use it on the Key to Rewards room on either the current floor or an earlier floor.

To the eighth floor

To the eighth floor

COMMON BATTLE CARDS

 Crabclaw

I should've known things would turn out this way.

MAP CARDS

 Almighty Darkness
 Looming Darkness
 Premium Room
 White Room
 Black Room
 Martial Waking
 Sorcerous Waking
 Alchemic Waking
 Meeting Ground
 Strong Initiative
 Lasting Daze
 Guarded Trove
 False Bounty
 Moment's Reprieve
 Moogle Room
 Key to Rewards

COMMON HEARTLESS

 Aquatank
 Darkball
 Screwdriver
 Sea Neon
 Search Ghost
Ursula (boss)

To the sixth floor

To the sixth floor

NEW SLEIGHTS

Homing Blizzara

Quake

Shock Impact

Spiral Wave

SPECIAL TREASURES IN ATLANTICA

You get two treasures from the Calm Bounty type rooms this time around: the sleights Shock Impact and Homing Blizzara. You can use Calm Bounty, Guarded Trove or False Bounty cards to open the two rooms needed to get both of these sleights. In the Key to Rewards room, you'll learn a third sleight, Quake.

Atlantica is the first and only underwater environment (Monstro doesn't count!) and it features unique underwater Heartless that you won't see anywhere else in the game. Even the basic Heartless icon is different here! Collect all of the enemy cards before leaving, unless you have a desire to return later.

Instead of Shadows, Atlantica features Sea Neons as the primary Heartless enemy. You'll get used to the new sprite quickly.

Ariel gladly helps out in battle whenever you visit Atlantica.

Because you are in the middle floors of the castle, normal battles are harder, longer, and more dangerous. The enemies are quick and smarter, too. You may notice that many of them can dodge sleights and long-range cards like Simba.

There is a good chance that when you use something like the Simba card, the enemies—especially the Screwdrivers, Search Ghosts, and Darkballs—will duck behind Sora at the last moment, putting themselves out of the attack's range.

Getting caught in the midst of these Heartless isn't a good idea. The Screwdrivers are swift and can inflict a lot of damage with their spears. Aquatanks, while slow and ungainly, are very dangerous when they let loose with their Thunder-based attacks. Until you get used to the flow of battle here in the deep, don't take your eyes off the Heartless, even to scroll between cards!

To help you in these battles, look for the **Crabclaw attack card** in the Treasure Spots. This Keyblade is a slightly better class than the ones encountered previously and will come in handy in battle. In addition, Ariel joins the party once you offer to help her in the Key of Guidance story room. Her attack is the swimming version of Goofy's dash attack.

THE CORAL SPIRES OF ATLANTICA

The most common Treasure Spot in Atlantica is one that you can only trigger by jumping down onto it. These Treasure Spots are the coral spires that you find all over the place. They are too tall for Sora to jump on and hitting them with a Keyblade does nothing. If you jump on top of one from a higher platform, however, prizes come flying out. Give it a try!

ARIEL

The daughter of king Triton who longs to see the outside world. Worried by Flounder's disappearance, Ariel was cajoled by Ursula into forking over the king's trident. We helped Ariel save Flounder and recover the trident, and she resolved to tell her father the truth.

FLOUNDER

A young fish. He's not exactly brave but Flounder is Ariel's most loyal friend. Ursula kidnapped Flounder as part of her plan to trick Ariel and steal the trident.

BOSS BATTLE URSULA

Ursula's thunder breath attack is quite powerful. It's a good thing that she rarely uses it!

If you opened Halloween Town on the sixth floor and the battle with Oogie Boogie is fresh in your mind, you'll enter this battle with a bit of an advantage. Ursula is another boss that fights with a bit of a pattern. After Ursula gets the trident, she quadruples in size. Protected by her tentacles, Ursula then proceeds to pelt Sora with lightning, confusion bubbles, and even thunder breath.

To counter her attacks, take out the tentacles (at least one) directly in front of her face. Although they regenerate after a short while, you have access to Ursula's face (her vulnerable spot) while they are gone. During this time, go after her with all you've got, hitting her with consecutive strikes of Sora's Keyblade. If you get a trick card during the battle, use it to bypass the tentacle slaying part and get immediate access to Ursula's face.

Take out at least one of the tentacles to get clear access to Ursula's weak spot—her face!

After depleting Ursula's health in half, she starts to move back and forth on the battlefield. Follow along and continue to fight when she pauses or stops. This is a great time to use any trick cards you may have acquired earlier in the fight.

DECK STRATEGIES

Come prepared to heal in this battle! Have at least two high-numbered Cure cards in your deck. A deck with lots of attack cards is also recommended. Once again, this is a battle in which you must destroy a barrier before you can inflict damage on the boss. Fighting with attack cards, as opposed to magic cards, provides more flexibility when fighting Ursula.

INTO THE CASTLE HALLS, BETWEEN THE SEVENTH AND EIGHTH FLOORS

Stop and save your game before entering the hallway between the seventh and eighth floors. A battle ensues when you run into one of Sora's best friends, Riku—but Riku is acting a bit strangely. He's not at all happy to see Sora…

BOSS BATTLE RIKU

Once stunned by Riku's triple attack, you'll need to wait until the effect wears off. This usually gives Riku enough time to unleash another attack.

You can pin down Riku while attacking him with relative ease. If you're having trouble doing so, take a look at your deck. You don't want any cards below 6 or 7.

Riku doesn't use any of his high-powered sleights in this fight. His most powerful attack is actually the third stroke of his triple sword attack. This blow has the power to stun Sora, leaving him paralyzed for a short time.

The best way to defeat Riku is to use a deck full of high-numbered attack cards. His speed is such that you need to let loose with streams of consecutive attacks without him card breaking you. If you give him an opening, he'll take it.

When you defeat Riku, you get the rare magic card, Aero. Heal at the save point and get ready to enter the eighth floor.

INSIDE THE BOSS'S DECK

Riku has three cards and three different attacks. Card "A" spawns a vertical slash attack; card "B" a dash and slash attack and card "C" a shake off-type attack. Riku has no sleights in this battle.

His deck is as follows:
"A" attack cards: 0 (x1); 2 (x1); 3 (x2); 4 (x2); 5 (x2); 6 (x2); 7 (x1); 9 (x1)
"B" attack cards: 0 (x1); 2 (x1); 3 (x2); 4 (x2); 5 (x2); 6 (x2); 7 (x1); 9 (x1)
"C" attack cards: 1 (x2); 4 (x1); 5 (x3); 6 (x1); 8 (x2)
Elixir: 5 (x1); 6 (x1)
Enemy card: Shadow

DECK STRATEGIES

Attack cards, attack cards, attack cards! Riku is fast at both attacking and dodging. Rely on Sora's Keyblade to win this fight.

CASTLE OBLIVION, EIGHTH FLOOR

At fourteen rooms, the eighth floor isn't any larger than the previous floor. In fact, floors seven through nine are all the same size; they're just arranged differently. There is really no distinct advantage or disadvantage to decide where to go to next.

The next default world is Never Land from the classic *Peter Pan*. This world is about equal to Atlantica in terms of level of activity and difficulty.

WORLD OPTIONS, EIGHTH FLOOR

 Atlantica

 Never Land

 Hollow Bastion

 Hundred Acre Wood

COMMON MAP CARDS

 Almighty Darkness

 Looming Darkness

 White Room

 Black Room

 Guarded Trove

FEATURED WORLD

The action in Never Land takes place entirely on Captain Hook's ship where Peter Pan is trying to rescue his friend Wendy. When Tinker Bell brings Sora to Peter to help, how can you say no? However, helping Peter means taking on Captain Hook…

NEW SLEIGHTS

Warpinator

WORLD MAP

EIGHTH FLOOR

NEVERLAND

NEVERLAND

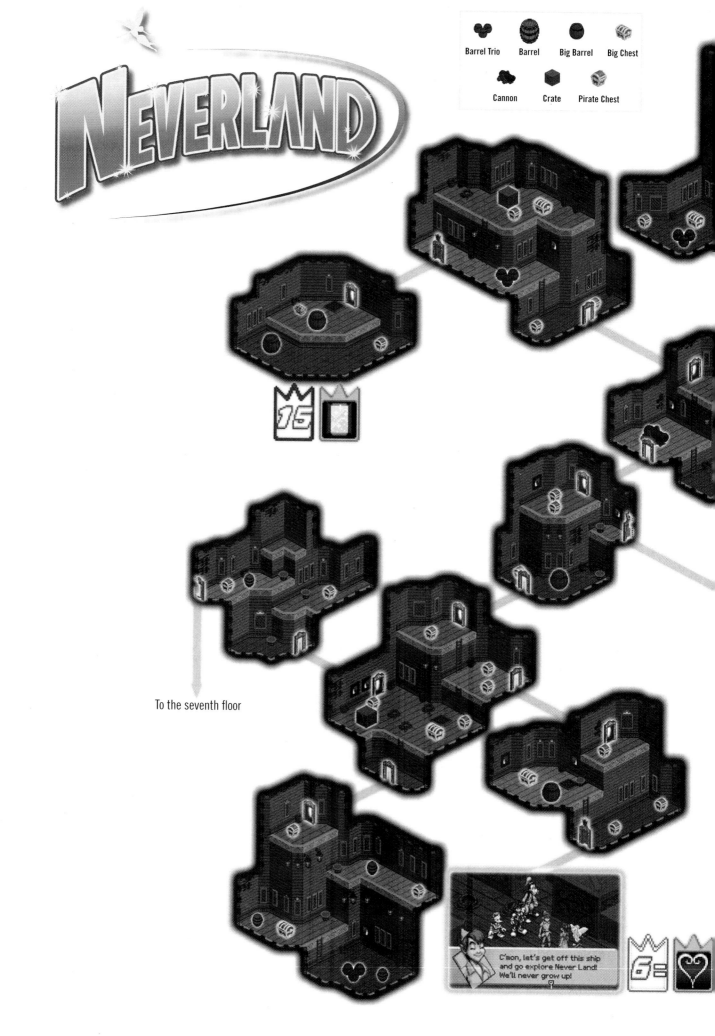

Barrel Trio   Barrel   Big Barrel   Big Chest

Cannon   Crate   Pirate Chest

To the seventh floor

C'mon, let's get off this ship and go explore Never Land! We'll never grow up!

To the ninth floor

I'll teach you to stow away on Captain Hook's vessel!

Is it just me, or are all the rooms starting to look the same?

NEW BATTLE CARDS

 Fairy Harp

 Tinker Bell

WELCOME TO
CASTLE OBLIVION

CHARACTERS

GAME BASICS

CASTLE
OBLIVION

MAP INFORMATION!

This sample map of Never Land was created using all Tranquil Darkness cards. While the rooms you create won't look the same as the ones here, the special door requirements and the layout of the floorplan are identical.

SPECIAL TREASURES IN NEVER LAND

Never Land is another world that gives you two prizes when you open up a second Calm Bounty/Guarded Trove/False Bounty room on the floor. Your two rewards this time are the sleights Teleport and Homing Fira. In the Key to Rewards room you'll learn another sleight, Thunder Raid.

COMMON HEARTLESS

 Air Pirate

 Air Soldier

 Barrel Spider

 Captain Hook (boss)

 Crescendo

 Darkball

 Gargoyle

 Pirate

 Shadow

 Yellow Opera

NEW SLEIGHTS

Homing Fira

Hummingbird

Teleport

Thunder Raid

Twinkle

MAP CARDS

 Almighty Darkness

 Looming Darkness

 Premium Room

 White Room

 Black Room

 Martial Waking

 Sorcerous Waking

 Alchemic Waking

 Meeting Ground

 Strong Initiative

 Lasting Daze

 Guarded Trove

False Bounty

Moment's Reprieve

 Moogle Room

 Key to Rewards

COOL TREASURE SPOTS IN NEVER LAND

The best Treasure Spot on Captain Hook's ship has to be the cannons. Hit them with Sora's Keyblade to make them shoot out prizes! It's a nice break from all of those barrels.

Two of the new Map Cards open rooms inhabited by very special Heartless. The White Room is home to the White Mushrooms. If you played the original *Kingdom Hearts*, then you should be familiar with these creatures. White Mushrooms are mischievous sprites that just want to play games. When you find one of them in each White Room, let the battle commence but don't attack the White Mushrooms. Instead, watch them and see what they do. If a White Mushroom shivers, blast it with Fire; if one starts fanning itself with its hands, cool it off with Blizzard. If one drops as if its battery has run out (look for the bolt over its head), use Thunder. This is the tactic to use against White Mushrooms on the battlefield and if you get three spells in a row correctly, the mushroom disappears. It will leave behind experience prizes, HP prizes, and possibly a premium prize (this is dropped by the first one you successfully help). To make this task easier, set up a specific deck with three or four of each type of magic card (Fire, Blizzard, and Thunder). If you're lucky, you may acquire the hard-to-find *White Mushroom card* at the end of a battle!

The Black Room is similar to the White Room, except this time you get to take on two groups of Black Funguses. Black Funguses are scrappy monsters that expel clouds of stun spores to paralyze their opponents. They also have an invulnerable side that is activated when they turn light gray in color. While the Black Fungus isn't impossible to kill, it does tend to take a while, especially when fighting a group of them. Your potential rewards include *Calm Bounty cards* or possibly the rare *Black Fungus card.*.

This time around all of the rooms look the same. So it should come as quite a relief to find out that the Heartless on this vessel are quite new and unique.

Agrabah had its bandits, Atlantica its Aquatanks and Sea Neons, and Never Land has its pirates. They attack from both the air and ground and each type has its own special nuances. The Air Pirates are fast and have the ability to stay just out of reach. Worse, though, are the normal Pirates. When one of their scimitars flashes, you'd better run! Their signature attack leaves Sora stunned and motionless for a decent period of time. To make matters worse, these Heartless like to attack in groups, making it difficult to escape this attack.

The stunning effect from the Pirates' attack lasts a long time, leaving Sora quite vulnerable to attack. If you get caught in a large group of Pirates, get ready to heal as soon as Sora regains his mobility.

Peter Pan attacks very much like Aerial and Goofy, using a quick dash across the battlefield. However, on your first trip through Never Land, you only get him for a short period of time.

As is standard for the worlds on the second through tenth floors, Never Land has its own unique Keyblade, the **Fairy Harp**. Don't rest until you find one, then find the Moogle Shop to acquire more. Peter Pan also joins the battle once you leave the Key of Beginnings story room. Of course, you lose him after the events in the Key of Guidance room, so explore the bulk of the rooms on this floor in-between those two events—especially if you like to use friend cards in battle.

PETER PAN

A boy who lives in Never Land, where no one ever grows up. Peter can be stubborn, but deep down he's brave and just. He was upset that Wendy wanted to return to London, but in the end he wished her well.

WENDY

A dreamy English girl. Peter showed her the way to Never Land. Wendy really likes Peter, but decided to return home to London.

HOOK

A pirate who holds a grudge against Peter Pan. Hook kidnapped Wendy to lure Peter out. Normally proud, Hook falls to pieces the moment the crocodile that took his hand shows up.

CAPTAIN HOOK

When Hook uses his "All Zeros" ability, it becomes more difficult to connect with a stream of attacks. After all, a zero card can break anything. And while it can still be broken by anything, his continued use of zero after zero card will override your attack cards. Instead, wait until he goes to recharge his deck, then hammer him into submission.

The ship's deck rocks back and forth, causing Sora to slide along with it.

The fight with Captain Hook is actually made easier if you're good at constantly pressing the A button. However, when you are recharging your deck or otherwise prevented from attacking, Hook can easily deplete Sora's HP gauge. Keep and eye on it and heal at the end of each round of cards.

Captain Hook is fast and has the rocking of the seas on his side. As the fight progresses, the ship's deck starts to rock back and forth, usually causing Sora to slide down the deck and into Hook's arms. Keep this in mind as you attempt to dodge attacks or heal.

Success in this battle is made simpler if you follow the "single opponent" strategy. Attack Hook with high-numbered cards, which will hopefully prevent him from card breaking you and interrupting your attack. When this boss goes to use a card combo or a deadly normal attack, pull out a zero card and card break his attack. An easy way to do this is to place at least one zero card at the start of your deck and then scroll past it at the start of the battle. When you see a big attack coming, simply use the Right Shoulder button to pull up the zero card, then launch it right after Captain Hook plays his hand.

Of course, you really want to card break the Rush & Present sleight before it starts...

Defeating Captain Hook gets you the standard boss enemy card. But before you leave, Tinker Bell hands over a present from Peter Pan—the Tinker Bell card.

DECK STRATEGIES

For this fight, put together the standard attack card deck. The vast majority of the attack cards in the deck should be high-numbered cards (7-9) and the rest should be zero attack cards. Use the high-numbered cards to keep up an unbreakable stream of hits and try to preserve the zero cards to card break Hook's special sleights. As always, your final slots should be 2-3 high-numbered Cure cards and a single Potion or Hi-Potion.

INSIDE THE BOSS'S DECK

Hook has a veritable treasure trove of attacks at his disposal. First of all, his deck is composed of four different attack cards which produce different attacks. The "A" card creates a thrusting attack, the "B" card a wild thrust, the "C" card a charging thrust, and "D" the punishing "present bomb" attack. His sleight Combo & Present is created when he stocks two "A" cards and a "C" card. Rush & Present is performed with the card combination of two "B" cards and one "C" card.

His deck is as follows:

"A" attack cards: 0 (x1); 1 (x1); 2 (x1); 3 (x1); 4 (x1); 5 (x1); 6 (x1); 7 (x1); 8 (x1); 9 (x1)

"B" attack cards: 0 (x1); 1 (x1); 2 (x1); 3 (x1); 4 (x1); 5 (x1); 6 (x1); 7 (x1); 8 (x1); 9 (x1)

"C" attack cards: 0 (x1); 1 (x1); 2 (x1); 3 (x1); 4 (x1); 5 (x1); 6 (x1); 7 (x1); 8 (x1); 9 (x1)

"D" attack cards: 0 (x1); 1 (x1); 2 (x1); 3 (x1); 4 (x1); 5 (x1); 6 (x1); 7 (x1); 8 (x1); 9 (x1)

Enemy cards: Hook, Sea Neon, Pirate

INTO THE CASTLE HALLS, BETWEEN THE EIGHTH AND NINTH FLOORS

Back in the hallway, it's time for another confrontation with Riku. This time, Sora instigates the battle.

RIKU

Dark Firaga is the latest addition to Riku's arsenal of attacks.

Riku isn't any harder (or easier) to defeat than he was the first time. The main difference is that now he likes to fight with combos, whether they're just three stacked cards or their sum is enough to launch his Dark Firaga sleight. Dark Firaga is a simple, dark fireball attack. It is easy to dodge by card breaking or just running out of the way.

Of course, the same cautions and strategies used in the first battle still hold true here. Keep Riku pinned down with streams of consecutive attacks and remember to heal often if he breaks loose. At the end of the battle, a card isn't given as a prize, but you do learn a new sleight, Warpinator.

DECK STRATEGIES

No changes to your deck are necessary here. The same cards that were used to fight Captain Hook on the eighth floor are appropriate against Riku.

INSIDE THE BOSS'S DECK

Riku's deck has grown but the number of different cards and basic attacks remains the same. New is the Dark Firaga sleight, which combines two "A" cards and a "C".

His deck is as follows:

"A" attack cards: 0 (x2); 1 (x1); 2 (x2); 3 (x2); 4 (x3); 5 (x3); 6 (x2); 7 (x2); 8 (x1); 9 (x2)

"B" attack cards: 0 (x2); 2 (x1); 3 (x1); 4 (x1); 5 (x1); 6 (x1); 7 (x1); 9 (x2)

"C" attack cards: 1 (x2); 4 (x2); 5 (x3); 6 (x2); 8 (x2)

Elixir: 4 (x1); 5 (x1); 6 (x1)

Enemy card: Shadow

CASTLE OBLIVION, NINTH FLOOR

The ninth floor is the last of the "easy" floors. Upon reaching the tenth floor, the floor plan increases to 17 rooms and the special room requirements soar. That's why it's highly recommended that you use the Hollow Bastion world card before you reach the tenth floor.

Hollow Bastion is possibly the most difficult world in the second group of world cards. Not only are the normal Heartless tough (those Defenders!), but the boss, Dragon Maleficent, is the most brutal boss you've fought so far. Save the Hundred Acre Wood map card for last and take care of Hollow Bastion here on the ninth floor.

WORLD OPTIONS, NINTH FLOOR

 Atlantica

 Never Land

 Hollow Bastion

 Hundred Acre Wood

COMMON MAP CARDS

 False Bounty

 Mingling Worlds

 Key to Rewards

FEATURED WORLD

In Hollow Bastion, you witness Belle coldly rejecting the Beast after he has come to rescue her from Maleficent's detention. The heart-broken Beast leaves in dispair. There must be a reason she is acting towards him in this way, but what could it be? It is up to you to find out.

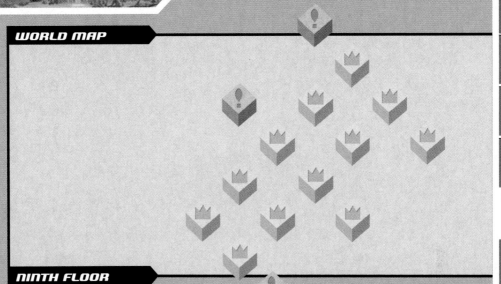

WORLD MAP

NINTH FLOOR

HOLLOW BASTION

HOLLOW BASTION

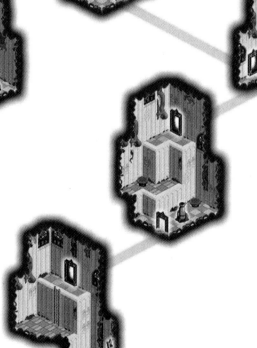

To the eighth floor

Column A   Column B   Column C   Column D   Obelisk   Steampipe   Tank

MAP INFORMATION!

This sample map of Hallow Bastion was created using all *Feeble Darkness cards*. While the rooms you create won't look the same as the ones here, the special door requirements and the layout of the floorplan are identical.

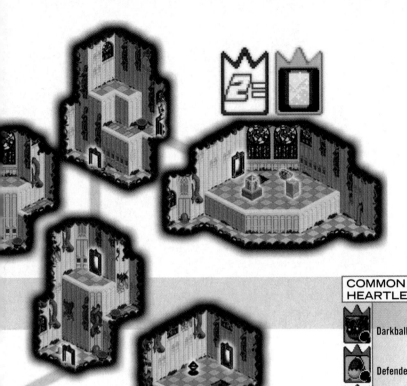

MAP CARDS

 Almighty Darkness

 Looming Darkness

 Premium Room

 White Room

 Black Room

 Martial Waking

 Sorcerous Waking

 Alchemic Waking

 Meeting Ground

 Strong Initiative

 Lasting Daze

 Guarded Trove

 False Bounty

 Moment's Reprieve

 Moogle Room

Key to Rewards

COMMON HEARTLESS

 Darkball

 Defender

 Dragon Maleficent (boss)

 Large Body

 Soldier

 Tornado Step

Wizard

Wyvern

To the tenth floor

What are you waiting for?
Call to him!

SPECIAL TREASURES IN HOLLOW BASTION

Hollow Bastion also rewards those who open up two Calm Bounty/
Guarded Trove/False Bounty rooms. The two prizes you'll find inside are
the sleights Omnislash and Reflect Raid. In the Key to Rewards room,
you'll find the summons card Mushu.

NEW SLEIGHTS

Omnislash

Ferocious Lunge

Flare Breath

Reflect Raid

Hollow Bastion is just plain difficult. From the moment you enter this world, prepare to be kicked around by Heartless of all shapes and sizes. New to the enemy list are the Defenders, Wizards, and those wiley Wyverns. Defenders are the highly armored version of the standard Large Bodies that you fought on the lower floors. These brutes bash Sora with their shields if you get too close and shoot fireballs as long-distance attacks. To make matters worse, they are surprisingly quick and can spin around to face you before you can get into position.

Wizards and Wyverns are also considerable threats. The Wizards float about the battlefield, casting high-level spells that can cause significant damage if you don't card break them at the start of casting. Wyverns have two attacks that you need to be aware of. Their dive attack pushes Sora from one side of the field to the other. This usually happens when you're trying to set up a combo and take your eyes of the action for a moment! The Wyvern's other attack involves repeatedly kicking Sora in the face and it is difficult to break this attack once it begins.

LOOKING FOR A CHALLENGE?

If you think that the Heartless on a floor aren't quite challenging enough, then open a room with the Almighty Darkness map card. Doing so creates a room in which all of the Heartless have high-numbered cards. This makes normal fights more like a boss-type fight.

The Beast takes the final slot in the Friends card list once you complete the Key of Guidance room. When Beast is summoned in battle, he races across the battlefield, mowing down any enemy that gets in his way. Also, the special Keyblade for the world is the powerful and fast **Divine Rose**.

The Beast attacks in the same manner as most of the other friends. He races across the battlefield knocking over the Heartless that get in his way.

The Defender's shield attack is very efficient at blocking your attempts to Dodge Roll past it. This makes it tough to get to its vulnerable backside.

When the Wyvern starts moving its legs like this, the opportunity to card break the attack is over. If this occurs, just grin and bear the attack.

BELLE

A young woman who saw kindness behind the Beast's gruff exterior. Realizing Maleficent sought her heart, Belle acted coldly toward the Beast to keep her heart beyond the witch's reach.

THE BEAST

A prince transformed into a beast because of his selfishness. Meeting Belle restored humanity to his heart. Though stunned by Belle's cold behavior, his faith in their love never wavered.

BOSS BATTLE DRAGON MALEFICENT

When Dragon Maleficent sends out a breath of flame, there's nowhere to hide!

When the attack ends, small piles of flame remain on the ground. Douse them with Sora's Keyblade to avoid taking any damage. These small fires are also where you'll find the helpful trick card.

Dragon Maleficent can be a really tough boss if you don't utilize the correct strategy. First, her attacks are limited to breath attacks and a nasty earthquake type attack when she slams her head against the floor. Her breath attacks cause a lot of damage, but Sora's Keyblade can be used to douse the pools of fire left behind by the attack. Additionally, this attack tends to spawn a friend card or a rare *trick card*. The quake attack is powerful and it takes time to recover from it, interrupting the flow of your attack.

To defeat Dragon Maleficent, unleash a flurry of constant attacks. Her vulnerable spot is her head, however, she keeps it on the edge of your attack range most of the time. When she does lower it, it signals that she's about to let loose with

Normally, you'd have to jump to reach Maleficent's weak spot. As long as you are connecting with consecutive hits, jumping is fine.

Using the trick card provides an advantage against Maleficent. As long as Sora is on the pile of bricks, Maleficent can't hurt him. If you jump down, though, she'll start to destroy the steps.

an attack. To bypass all of the jumping and card breaking required to actually hit the Dragon, use the trick card. These are pretty easy to get in this battle and when you use one it drops a handy concrete block beneath Dragon Maleficent's head. All you have to do is jump on it and start hitting her!

As always, keep an eye on Sora's health as you carry out your attacks. It is very easy to go from full health to close to no health when Maleficent starts breathing fire.

DECK STRATEGIES

For this battle, bring out your attack card deck and update it with any new cards you have acquired while in Hallow Bastion. Basically, you want the majority of the attack cards to be 8 or 9 cards and the remainder as zero cards. Put three to four Cure cards and the standard Potion/Hi-Potion card at the end of the deck.

INTO THE CASTLE HALLS, BETWEEN THE NINTH AND TENTH FLOORS

After three exciting hallway battles, the hallway between the ninth and tenth floors is quiet and peaceful. However, the situation for Sora and his friends isn't so uneventful as their memories continue to unravel and you learn more about the Organization in charge of the Castle.

CASTLE OBLIVION, TENTH FLOOR

The tenth floor reveals a hint of what's to come as you near the final three castle floors. Not only is this floor *huge*, the special door requirements are much higher than previous floors.

The default world for this floor is the Hundred Acre Wood. It is a completely different type of world than any of the others before it. It has no Heartless or bosses, just Pooh and his friends in one large room. This world makes a great break from the heavy-duty fighting, leveling up, and card maintenance up to this point.

WORLD OPTIONS, TENTH FLOOR

 Atlantica

 Never Land

 Hallow Bastion

 Hundred Acre Wood

COMMON BATTLE CARDS

 Mega-Ether

FEATURED WORLD

The Hundred Acre Wood is not exempt from the memory-erasing powers of Castle Oblivion and Pooh is feeling the effects. Your job is to take Pooh around the world and reunite him with six of his "bestest" friends. Are you up for the challenge?

COMMON MAP CARDS

False Bounty

Mingling Worlds

Key to Rewards

WORLD MAP

TENTH FLOOR

100 HUNDRED ACRE WOOD

MR SANDERS

RNIG ALSO

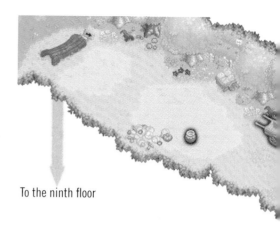

To the ninth floor

WINNIE THE POOH

A bear who lives in the base of a tree in the Hundred Acre Wood. Pooh loves to eat—especially honey. He's gentle and easygoing, but a little absent-minded.

PIGLET

Pooh's closest friend. Piglet is very shy and when he's surprised he covers his eyes with his floppy ears.

TIGGER

The one and only. Cheerful Tigger loves to bounce all day long. Sometimes his energy is too much for the others, but he always means well.

OWL

The wisest animal in the Hundred Acre Wood. Sometimes he talks so much his friends fall asleep.

ROO

A feisty kangaroo who's full of energy. Little Roo wants to learn to bounce as high as Tigger.

EEYORE

A gloomy donkey whose tail keeps falling off and getting lost.

RABBIT

A diligent gardener who's always busy with his vegetables. Sometimes Rabbit is a bit short-tempered, especially when Tigger bounces around his garden.

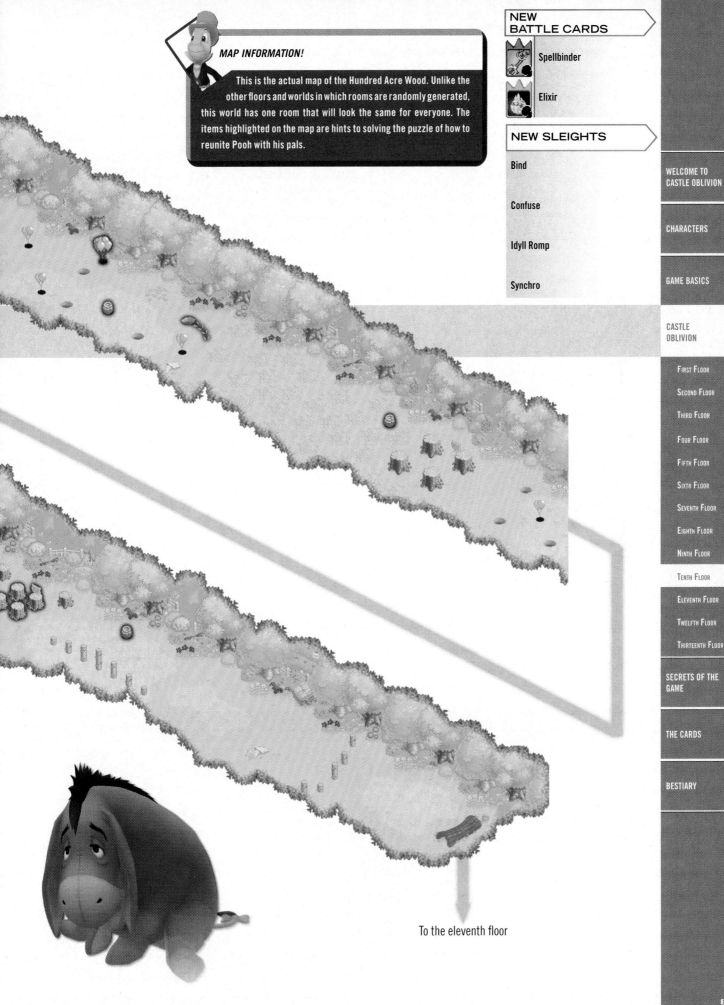

MAP INFORMATION!

This is the actual map of the Hundred Acre Wood. Unlike the other floors and worlds in which rooms are randomly generated, this world has one room that will look the same for everyone. The items highlighted on the map are hints to solving the puzzle of how to reunite Pooh with his pals.

NEW BATTLE CARDS

Spellbinder

Elixir

NEW SLEIGHTS

Bind

Confuse

Idyll Romp

Synchro

To the eleventh floor

Since the sample map doesn't have any story rooms associated with it, here are the requirements for the three story rooms and the Key to Rewards room:

Key of Beginnings Room	Key of Guidance Room	Key to Truth Room	Key to Rewards Room
3↓ ↑	7↑ ♡	0= ♡	3= 7=

JUST A GENTLE REMINDER!

If you choose to go with the Hundred Acre Wood for the tenth floor, there are no enemies to fight so you won't receive any map or enemy cards. In addition, there are no Treasure Spots in the Hundred Acre Wood, so you won't find any cards or HP prizes either. However, the quest in the Hundred Acre Wood rewards you with some fabulous things, so you're not missing out on anything!

As noted previously, the Hundred Acre Wood is a unique place. The goal here is to lead Pooh to his friends and determine how to reunite them. Sometimes all you need to do is lead Pooh directly to the friend to make them reconnect. Other pals are busy doing their own thing and won't stop to make time for Pooh unless you figure out a way to get their attention. To make Pooh follow Sora, walk closely in front of him. If something captures his attention (like butterflies), wave to him by pressing the R Button. This works only if you are nearby, less than half a screen away.

The other concern is keeping Pooh supplied with enough honey to keep him fit and mobile. The gauge in the upper-right corner of the screen monitors Pooh's Honey Level. If it reaches zero, Pooh needs to take a nap until he recovers a small portion of his health (equal to one-third of the honey pot). When this level is achieved, wake him up and lead him to one of the honey pots located in convenient spots throughout the woods.

Sora and Pooh have something in common: They are both looking for friends they have shadowy memories of.

Feeding Pooh is one of Sora's most important duties! Try to hit every honey pot you find. Don't worry about wasting them; the honey pots regenerate after a short period of time.

PIGLET

Piglet is the easiest of the six friends to find. He's located just to the south of where Rabbit is moving his cabbages and carrots. Simply get Pooh close to his friend and an event automatically occurs. At the end of the reunion, Piglet relinquishes the sleight, **Confuse**.

Why, hello there, Piglet.

To trigger the reunion event with Piglet, simply get Pooh close to him.

OWL

Next, look for a bunch of balloons near a tree along the northern wall of the trail and beckon Pooh to the balloons. This is more difficult than it looks, as Pooh is drawn to both the smaller group of balloons and the butterflies that litter the landscape. However, with enough waving and careful positioning of Sora, you can get him to grab the balloons and soar into the air. When he flies too high, his old pal Owl jumps into the air and rescues him. The reward for setting up this event is the **Spellbinder attack card**.

Keep Pooh away from the butterflies and he'll eventually grab the balloons near the tree where Owl roosts. When he goes too high into the sky, it's Owl to the rescue!

ROO

Further down the path, at the end of the second group of holes and balloons, there's a hole with footprints leading up to it. Lead Pooh to the hole and let him fall in. When he floats out of the hole—thanks to the helium balloons hidden inside—he's not alone. Roo emerges from the hole with him. For triggering this meeting, Roo hands over the **Elixir item card**.

The footprints are a dead giveaway that you should investigate this hole. Were you surprised when Roo appeared, holding onto Pooh's legs?

TIGGER

Tigger is totally wrapped up in hopping from stump to stump. However, if you lead Pooh further down the path you'll find Roo sitting by a group of tree stumps that look remarkably like the ones Tigger's playing on. Coax Pooh onto one of them, then make him jump from one stump to the other, imitating Tigger. When done correctly, Tigger immediately comes over to investigate. It seems that imitation truly is the sincerest form of flattery where Tigger is concerned and as a reward you learn the sleight, **Idyll Romp**.

Pooh is an eager student, especially when it comes to something as fun as jumping. Just position Sora next to the stump you want Pooh to jump to and press the R Button to wave to him.

Eeyore is too concerned about his missing tail to pay Pooh much mind. Your job is to find a way to get Eeyore's tail out of the tree where it's stuck and back to its owner. To accomplish this feat, look for a small beehive in a tree along the north wall to the south of Eeyore. When you bring Pooh nearby, his curiosity disturbs the bees causing them to chase him across the field and right into the tree with Eeyore's tail. The resulting impact knocks the tail out of the tree and back into Eeyore's hooves. Once his tail is back in place, Eeyore is more than willing to talk to his old pal. Completing this task earns Sora the sleight, **Bind**. Now, only one friend remains.

Those bees do not look happy, but this little disturbance has great effects.

RABBIT

When you first run into Rabbit at the start of the trail, he's too busy with his produce to bother with Sora or Pooh. Just north of where he's working, look for a rickety wagon. Motion Pooh inside and then make Sora get in. If you move around, the wagon breaks. Oops!

Continue down the road picking up all of the other characters. As you journey past the stumps where you finally met up with Tigger, a strange thing occurs: Cabbages start rolling down the road. Hit them with Sora's Keyblade to make them fall into a neat pile by the side of the road. You need to hit 14 cabbages (forming a neat pyramid). After doing so, Rabbit appears, overjoyed with the help you've provided. As a reward for getting these two friends back together, Sora learns the sleight, **Synchro**.

Once you've reunited Pooh with all six of his friends, lead him to the end of the trail. From here you can choose to exit the Hundred Acre Wood and continue with the bigger quest. Don't forget to save when prompted!

Don't worry! This innocent vandalism is key to reuniting Pooh with Rabbit.

Hit the cabbages as they roll by to knock them into a neat pile. Complete the pile and Rabbit shows up to check on his produce.

As soon as you enter the hallways between the tenth and eleventh floors, you run into Vexen. It's time for another boss fight. If you chose to go with the Hundred Acre Wood for the tenth floor world, then you should be ready to do some fighting!

BOSS BATTLE VEXEN

Vexen is the person responsible for the Riku replica. Fortunately, this battle isn't too difficult if you are quick on your feet. Vexen carries a large ice shield that protects him from frontal assaults, kind of like the Defenders and Large Body enemies. Therefore, you need to position Sora behind Vexen and stay there. This enables you to inflict damage on him while staying away from his attacks. If you approach him from the front, you will likely get caught in his Freeze spell or cuffed by his shield.

When you sustain damage, use the Cure cards that should be at the end of your deck. At the end of the battle, you win a *Mega-Ether* item card. Vexen also relinquishes the next *world card*, one forged from your deepest memories.

The easiest way to take down Vexen is to pursue him from behind with Sora's Keyblade. Your cards should be at a high enough level to defend against most of his attacks.

Vexen's Freeze attack is extremely powerful. The longer that Sora stays frozen, the more damage he incurs. Dodge the attack or use a zero card to card break it.

If you stand in front of Vexen, there's a good chance that he'll smack Sora with his shield. This doesn't do a lot of damage but it will knock Sora to the ground, delaying a counterattack.

DECK STRATEGIES

A standard boss deck should be enough to take Vexen down. Ultimately, it depends on what—or who—you last fought. If Dragon Maleficent was your last opponent, then your deck should be in good shape. Remember, at this point, you want your deck to contain attack cards at levels zero and 9. About a 50-50 mix of each number will suffice.

INSIDE THE BOSS'S DECK

Vexen has two types of cards, one magic and one physical attack. The blue card "A" produces the attack Blizzara and red card "B" produces Vexen's shield blow attack. His sleight Freeze is produced by stocking Card "A" + Card "B" + Card "A".

His deck is as follows:
"A" attack cards: 0 (x3); 1 (x1); 2 (x3); 3 (x1); 7 (x3); 8 (x1); 9 (x2)
"B" attack cards: 0 (x2); 1 (x3); 2 (x1); 3 (x3); 7 (x1); 8 (x1); 9 (x3)
Mega-Ether: 3 (x1); 4 (x1); 5 (x1); 6 (x1)
Elixir: 0 (x1); 1 (x1); 8 (x1); 9 (x1)
Enemy card: Blue Rhapsody

CASTLE OBLIVION, ELEVENTH FLOOR

The final three worlds in *Kingdom Hearts: Chain of Memories* are actually assigned to specific floors. On the eleventh floor, you revisit Twilight Town, a place created from Sora's memories that he is having trouble remembering. The task here is to help Sora unravel his memories about a certain girl and a certain promise.

RIKU

Sora's childhood friend. Baited by the darkness and used by Maleficent and Ansem, Riku once fought against Sora. In order to seal the door to darkness, Riku stayed with the king on the other side. His current whereabouts are unknown. Sora journeys in the hopes of finding Riku.

VEXEN

A man absorbed in his dubious research in Castle Oblivion. Vexen tried to destroy Sora by controlling Riku and pitting the two against each other. When this plan failed, he confronted Sora personally.

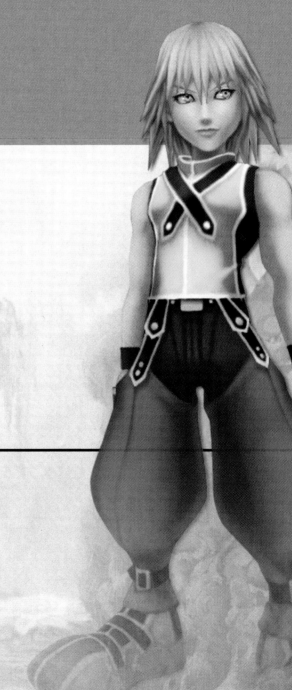

FEATURED WORLD

SPECIAL TREASURES IN TWILIGHT TOWN

This is an unusual world in that you have three different treasures to find. The first is the standard Calm Bounty treasure. This time you get the sleight Firaga Break. In the Key to Rewards room look for the sleight Warp.

That leaves us with the third item. The One-Winged Angel remains hidden ~~in~~ world until you defeat Marluxia for the first time in Castle Oblivion. ~~You c~~an come back here and find it in a Treasure Spot.

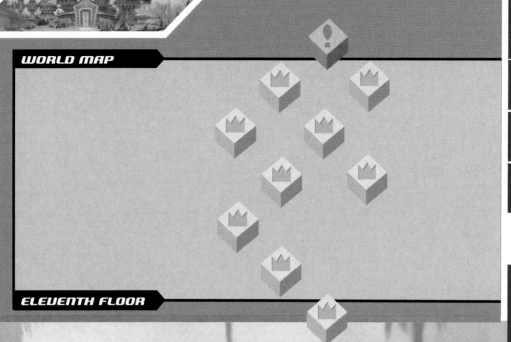

WORLD MAP

ELEVENTH FLOOR

Twilight Town

To the tenth floor

Barrel	Boxes	Flowerbox	Lamp

MAP INFORMATION!

This is a sample map of Twilight Town. This map was created using all *Premium Room cards*. While the rooms you create probably won't look the same as the ones here, the special door irements and the layout of the floorplan are identical.

I'm sure I don't know this place, but it's starting to feel real familiar...

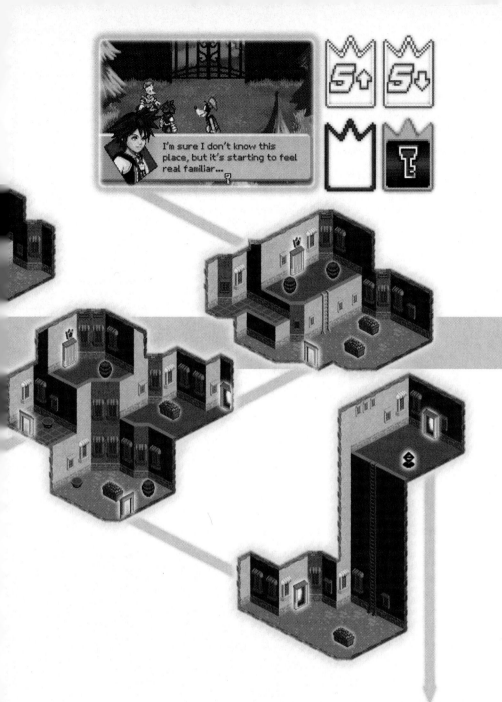

To the twelfth floor

To the twelfth floor

COMMON HEARTLESS

- Air Soldier
- Barrel Spider
- Riku (boss)
- Shadow
- Soldier
- Vexen (boss)

MAP CARDS

 Almighty Darkness

 Looming Darkness

 Premium Room

 White Room

 Black Room

 Martial Waking

 Sorcerous Waking

 Alchemic Waking

 Meeting Ground

 Strong Initiative

 Lasting Daze

 Guarded Trove

 False Bounty

 Moment's Reprieve

 Moogle Room

 Key to Rewards

COMMON BATTLE CARDS

 Mega Potion

 One-Winged Angel

NEW SLEIGHTS

Firaga Break

Warp

Twilight Town takes you back to the basics with battles full of Shadows, Soldiers, and Air Soldiers. However, these Heartless are a lot more powerful than the ones you fought back on the lower floors. Their attacks may be the same, but they have much more power and longer HP gauges.

Fighting in Twilight Town is like deja vu all over again!

At this point in the game, you should know the sleights Shock Impact and Ragnarok. Shock Impact is obtained from a Calm Bounty room in Atlantica and requires the use of a Simba card plus any two attack cards. When used in battle, this sends a shockwave across the field, pinning and stunning any foes against the far wall.

Shock Impact takes the Simba card to a whole new level!

Ragnarok is a sleight that is learned through leveling up. It requires three attack cards whose sum equals between 2 to 9. Ragnarok causes Sora to fire a large stream of laser rays from his Keyblade across the battlefield.

If you are nimble and quick enough at stocking and sending sleights, you can use these two in combination to great effect. Use Shock Impact first to send all of the Heartless on the battlefield to the other side of the field. Then, quickly stock and send Ragnarok to blast them before the stun effect of Shock Impact wears off and they have the chance to evade Ragnarok's rays. If you like the way this works, set the combos up ahead of time in your deck.

Twilight Town is unusual because it only has a single story room. What this means is that when you enter it, you should be prepared for a boss fight. You should also take note that the prices in a Moogle Shop (once you open one) have risen once again. These prices stay in effect from the eleventh floor to the thirteenth floor.

Heartless are very good at evading Ragnarok's blast by rushing to stand behind Sora when he casts it. So, trick them by casting it while you are in the middle of the battlefield. Then, right when the attack is about to take place, pull Sora back to the end of the field to include all of the Heartless standing in front of him.

Example of a Shock Impact/Ragnarok deck.

MOOGLE SHOP
MOOGLE POINTS
00379

200 Points
250 Points
270 Points
300 Points

Ouch! The new price of cards will have you scrambling for more Moogle Points if you want to buy them all!

BOSS BATTLE VEXEN

This time around, Vexen is more difficult to defeat. During the first encounter, it was easy to dodge his attacks or sneak up behind him to attack his vulnerable backside. Now Vexen can defend against this approach, spinning around to face Sora the moment he tries to attack from behind.

Vexen's bag of tricks has also grown since the last encounter. He's learned two new sleights (Ice Needles and Iceburn) in addition to his Freeze iceburg. Ice Needles calls forth a line of ice needles from the ground. The line of ice follows Sora around the battlefield until you card break the attack or are hit by the frozen shards. Iceburn creates pools of slippery ice on the ground that hinders Sora's movement. Card breaking is key to survival against these attacks.

It's tough to get Vexen to stand still long enough to actually hit him with an attack. Most of the time, he spins around just in time to block Sora's Keyblade attacks.

Iceburn is an unusual attack. It can be quite tricky to avoid, especially if Vexen levitates over to the other side of the battlefield, leaving you to run over the slippery ice slicks.

Ice Needles is Vexen's most aggressive attack. Those shards of ice can—and will—follow Sora anywhere on the battlefield.

To win this bout, you must break Vexen's attacks while Dodge Rolling around to his back to deliver your own attacks. He uses combo attacks much of the time, so have at least one—if not two—zero cards tucked away at the front of your deck and use them immediately after he starts a combo. If not, you will likely find yourself in a world of hurt after getting hit with Freeze or Ice Needles a couple of times!

DECK STRATEGIES

Make sure that your deck has a few more zero cards than usual. Vexen uses a lot of sleights and it is important to have zero cards on hand to break them. Try using a 50-50 split between high-numbered attack cards and zero attack cards. Follow them with 3-4 Cure cards and a Potion/Hi-Potion.

INSIDE THE BOSS'S DECK

Vexen's deck hasn't changed much since your battle in the hallway. This time you have two new sleights to deal with. You can tell Iceburn is coming when Vexen starts stocking 2 "A" cards and a "B". Ice Needles uses all "A" cards.

His deck is as follows:
"A" attack cards: 0 (x3); 1 (x2); 2 (x3); 3 (x1); 7 (x3); 8 (x2); 9 (x3)
"B" attack cards: 0 (x3); 1 (x3); 2 (x1); 3 (x3); 7 (x1); 8 (x2); 9 (x3)
Mega-Ether: 2 (x1); 3 (x1); 4 (x1); 5 (x1); 6 (x1)
Elixir: 0 (x1); 1 (x1); 5 (x1); 7 (x1); 8 (x1); 9 (x1)
Enemy cards: Vexen, Blue Rhapsody, Air Pirate

INTO THE CASTLE HALLS, BETWEEN THE ELEVENTH AND TWELFTH FLOORS

BOSS BATTLE RIKU (BATTLE #3)

Again, the same rules apply in this battle that you used in the last two against Riku. Attack, attack, attack!

It's time for another battle against Riku. Expect this fight to be a bit tougher than the last one, as Riku has a few more tricks up his sleeve. As always, victory comes from your ability to card break his attacks while connecting with uninterrupted streams of Sora's attacks.

Victory against Riku this time nets you a **Mega-Potion** card and the next world card. But it also raises some serious concerns in the minds of your companions, as you proceed to the entrance of the twelfth floor.

DECK STRATEGIES

The deck you used against Vexen should work just fine against Riku.

INSIDE THE BOSS'S DECK

A fourth card and basic attack have been added to Riku's deck for this battle. The "D" card allows Riku to perform a head blow-type attack.

His deck is as follows:
"A" attack cards: 0 (x2); 1 (x1); 2 (x1); 3 (x2); 4 (x3); 5 (x3); 6 (x2); 7 (x1); 8 (x1); 9 (x2)
"B" attack cards: 0 (x2); 4 (x3); 5 (x3); 9 (x2)
"C" attack cards: 1 (x2); 4 (x3); 5 (x3); 8 (x2)
"D" attack cards: 1 (x1); 2 (x2); 3 (x1); 4 (x1); 5 (x1); 6 (x1); 7 (x2); 8 (x1)
Elixir: 4 (x1); 5 (x2); 6 (x1)
Enemy card: Shadow

CASTLE OBLIVION, TWELFTH FLOOR

There are two main things to keep in mind regarding the twelfth floor, Destiny Islands. First is the fact that you cannot call upon Donald or Goofy while you're in the Destiny Islands world. This ban holds even after you've cleared the floor and return after completing the events of the thirteenth floor.

Second, there are only two story rooms on this floor. The first one contains the standard cut-scene, while the second one holds this world's boss battle.

SPECIAL TREASURES IN DESTINY ISLANDS

Destiny Islands holds the final Key to Rewards room in the game and the prize, the Megalixir item card, is worth the wait. And don't forget to grab the Judgment sleight from a Calm Bounty room before you leave.

FEATURED WORLD

The Destiny Islands are, of course, Sora's homeland and the return here should be bittersweet, spurring a flood of memories. Instead, Sora is fixated on one thing: finding out the truth behind his shared memory with Riku. If it sounds like you should anticipate yet another battle with the angry Riku, the answer is yes. However, it doesn't happen until you clear the floor and exit into the Hallway. This gives you a little bit of time to prepare—and prepare you should!

At this point in the game, with two floors left, things really heat up! If you haven't spent a lot of extra time leveling Sora up or collecting all of the cards and sleights, now is a good time to start.

You may consider returning to the first six floors and take some time to open all of the Key to Rewards rooms, verify that you have all of the Calm Bounty treasures for those floors, and collect any missing enemy cards. All of this work should level up Sora quite a bit. Concentrate on boosting his CP. For the Riku battle ahead, try getting Sora to around 400 HP or so, which is three-fourths of his max total.

er Moogle Points and use them to purchase cards on the lower floors where card packs are cheaper. Before you leave the twelfth floor, erative that your deck consists largely of attack cards of good strength (i.e. solid mid-level Keyblades) with high numbers (preferably zero, 9 only).

WORLD MAP

TWELFTH FLOOR

DESTINY ISLANDS

DESTINY ISLANDS

To the thirteenth floor

To the thirteenth floor

MAP INFORMATION!

This sample map of Destiny Islands was created using all *Meeting Ground cards*. While the rooms you create won't look the same as the ones here, the special door requirements and the layout of the floorplan are identical.

To the eleventh floor

Oathkeeper

 Oblivion

 Almighty Darkness

 Looming Darkness

 Premium Room

 White Room

 Black Room

 Guarded Trove

 False Bounty

 Moment's Reprieve

 Moogle Room

 Mingling Worlds

 Key to Rewards

 Barrel Spider

 Creeper Plant

 Crescendo

 Darkball

 Darkside (boss)

 Replica Riku (boss)

 Shadow

 Tornado Step

Judgment

Barrel	Big Bush	Bush	Crate	Plant	Tree

Hey, Sora. What's the big rush?

The island's breaking up!

Aim for the Darkside's head. If you can card break all of his attacks, it's the only target you'll ever see.

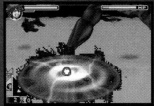

You can jump to miss the shockwave entirely if you want to dodge it manually. If not, just card break it when you see the Darkside start to bend down.

The Darkside follows a fairly set pattern. It's main vulnerable spot is its face, which is accessible only about half of the time. You can also target its hand after a particular attack, but it's easier to card break the attack and work against a single target.

The Darkside has three main attacks. The first is a shockwave type attack that erupts when he slams his fist against the ground. There is a second form to this attack in which the Darkside actually plunges his arm deep into the sand.

The second and third attacks use homing energy balls to inflict their damage. You'll come to recognize these from their starting stance (in one case, Darkside fires an energy ball from his hands, and in the other he fires the energy ball from his chest) and know when to card break them. You can dodge them manually, but

In this attack, the Darkside sends an energy ball into the sky where it explodes into a rain shower of dark energy.

In this attack, the Darkside shoots a homing energy ball out of his chest.

it's a lot easier to card break them out of existence.

The good thing about the Darkside is that he has no combo attacks, so card breaking is fairly easy, even if you don't have a zero card immediately on hand. The main thing you have to physically combat is the wind, which continuously blows Sora from right to left. To counteract the wind, work from the right side of the screen at the Darkside's feet.

There are two postures from which to attack the Darkside. The first is the "volleyball" pose used to begin one of the energy ball attacks. This one doesn't last long after you card break the attack, but you can jump onto the Darkside's arms and get in a few hits. The second opening comes when the Darkside buries his arm into the sand. This pose lasts a little longer, but you need to keep Sora from locking onto the Shadows that spawn from the sand. If you can do that, you can take the Darkside's HP gauge down at least one-third before he stands back up again.

When the Darkside buries his right arm in the sand, jump up and start hitting his head.

Alternatively, you can try to get a few hits in after card breaking the Darkside's energy ball attack.

Sometimes, you can get a couple of strikes in after card breaking the Darkside's other energy ball attack.

Ultimately, this is a long battle because the Darkside spends half of the time out of attack range. Be patient and you'll eventually win this battle. At the end of the battle, you get the **Darkside card** and at the end of the cut-scene you get the **Oathkeeper attack card**.

INTO THE CASTLE HALLS, BETWEEN THE TWELFTH AND THIRTEENTH FLOORS

Once again, you get to battle Riku. This is the final battle against this particular foe and it's a hard one if you don't come prepared. After this fight, return to the save point and save your game. The reason for this is that there's another fight after this one, even before you reach the end of the hallway.

BOSS BATTLE RIKU (BATTLE #4)

In his Dark Aura attack, Riku jets around the battlefield and homes in on Sora's position. The duration of this attack is remarkably long, so if you get stuck in it, scroll through your deck until you find a zero card to card break it.

This is probably the toughest battle thus far. Riku is TOUGH. He now uses his Dark Aura attack, which can take Sora from a full HP gauge to almost empty in 30 seconds, unless you card break the attack first. You'll need to card break to win this battle, too. Keep a zero card or two at the start of your deck and move them out the way, in the R Button position as noted previously. Use them only to card break Dark Aura.

Riku's attacks are also fast and hard to deflect. He also has the ability to break Sora's attacks easily. Add to that his amazing speed and you'll find yourself sweating to keep up with him. But if you can pin Riku into a corner—especially when he's trying to reload his deck—you can inflict some serious damage. Riku has three HP bars, so prepare for a long fight.

INSIDE THE BOSS'S DECK

Dark Aura is the only new attack to join Riku's repertoire in this final battle. Dark Aura is made up of a combination of two "B" cards and a "D".
His deck is as follows:
"A" attack cards: 0 (x2); 1 (x2); 3 (x2); 4 (x3); 5 (x3); 6 (x2); 8 (x2); 9 (x2)
"B" attack cards: 0 (x2); 1 (x2); 2 (x1); 3 (x2); 4 (x3); 5 (x3); 6 (x2); 7 (x1); 8 (x2); 9 (x2)
"C" attack cards: 1 (x1); 2 (x1); 3 (x1); 4 (x2); 5 (x2); 6 (x2); 7 (x1); 8 (x1)
"D" attack cards: 0 (x1); 1 (x2); 2 (x2); 7 (x2); 8 (x2); 9 (x1)
Elixir: 4 (x1); 5 (x2); 6 (x1); 9 (x1)
Enemy card(s): Shadow, Riku

BOSS BATTLE LARXENE

Teleport Rush is Larxene's new attack. Here she warps around the battlefield, hitting Sora with balls of lightning.

After the Riku fight, return to Destiny Islands and save your game. This replenishes Sora's HP and prevents you from having to redo the Riku battle if you don't fare well in the next fight.

Larxene is a Thunder girl and, like lightning, she strikes fast and hard. However, compared to Riku, she's doesn't put up a strong fight. Larxene still uses the Lightning Bolt sleight and the two "normal" Thunder attacks from the first fight. New to the battle, though, is her Teleport Rush sleight, which enables her to warp around the battlefield, hitting Sora with lightning orbs.

Fortunately, Larxene's Teleport Rush is nowhere near as dangerous as Riku's Dark Aura. If you keep up the card breaks and solid attacks, you should have no problem defeating Larxene. To make things easier, Goofy and Donald both return at the start of the battle, bringing the return of the friend cards.

DECK STRATEGIES

Focus on the number of zero cards in your deck. If you have too many zero cards, Riku will constantly card break Sora. If you have too few, he will decimate Sora with his combo attacks. Use an approximately 70-30% ratio from the deck used against the Darkside when going into this battle, making sure to keep at least one zero card tucked away at the beginning of your deck for emergencies. If you've only been keeping 3-4 Cure cards in your deck, you might want to up the number by one or two. You'll need them to cast Cura or Curaga at the end of each card round.

INSIDE THE BOSS'S DECK

Larxene has two new attacks in this battle. First up is her angry rush attack, which is activated whenever she is close to death. In fact this attack takes the place of the Thundara assigned to her blue "C" card. The other is a new sleight called Teleport Rush, which is summoned with 2 "B" cards and an 'A' card.

Her deck is as follows:
"A" attack cards: 0 (x2); 1 (x2); 3 (x2); 4 (x2); 5 (x2); 6 (x2); 7 (x2); 8 (x2); 9 (x2)
"B" attack cards: 0 (x2); 1 (x2); 3 (x2); 4 (x2); 5 (x2); 6 (x2); 7 (x2); 8 (x2); 9 (x2)
"C" attack cards: 0 (x2); 2 (x2); 4 (x2); 6 (x2); 8 (x2)
Elixir: 3 (x1); 6 (x1)
Enemy card(s): Larxene, Yellow Opera

CASTLE OBLIVION, THIRTEENTH FLOOR

You've finally reached the top of Castle Oblivion. The thirteenth floor may not be the luckiest, but it's all that stands between you and the end of the game.

SPECIAL TREASURES IN CASTLE OBLIVION

The true treasures on this floor are well hidden. The first is the Diamond Dust attack card. It can be found in Treasure Spots once you defeat Marluxia. The second is a set of treasures that only becomes available after you clear the Riku Mode game. Once you defeat Riku's final boss, come back to this floor and start opening Calm Bounty rooms. You'll need to open three to get the Ultima Weapon, the Lexaeus enemy card and the Ansem enemy card—which should fill the three empty slots in your Journal!

FEATURED WORLD

Castle Oblivion (the world) is *huge*! The format of the floor plan is such that you must visit almost every room on your way to the single story room and the Hallway beyond. Save point strategies are very important, as are healing strategies. Since the normal battles here in Castle Oblivion are longer and tougher than any you've fought before, it is important that you rearrange your deck to include at least another Cure card.

Once again, time spent leveling up before you really attack this floor is time well spent. It is recommended that you fully plunder the first six floors and do the same for the last six. Again, open up any Key to Rewards rooms you might have neglected and check for any missing Calm Bounty treasures. Collect the remaining enemy cards and you should be good to go.

The most difficult of the enemy cards to collect is possibly the White Mushroom and Black Fungus cards. Since you can't fight these creatures in rooms that increase your chance of getting enemy cards, you'll have to do it the hard way. First, make sure you have a decent supply of White and Black room cards (three to four of each should suffice). Then head down to one of the middle floors and save your game at the Hallway save point and head into the world you've chosen. Open nothing but White and Black Rooms and defeat the two groups of Heartless. If you fail to get one of the enemy cards in any of the rooms you opened, reboot and reload your game to start again.

Before you take Sora back to the thirteenth floor, make sure that his level is somewhere in the 70s and that you've maxed out his HP at 540HP.

WORLD MAP

THIRTEENTH FLOOR

MARLUXIA

Lord of Castle Oblivion and a member of the Organization. In a move to bring the group under his control, Marluxia used Namine to overrun Sora's memory and tried to claim the power of the Keyblade.

CASTLE OBLIVION

CASTLE OBLIVION

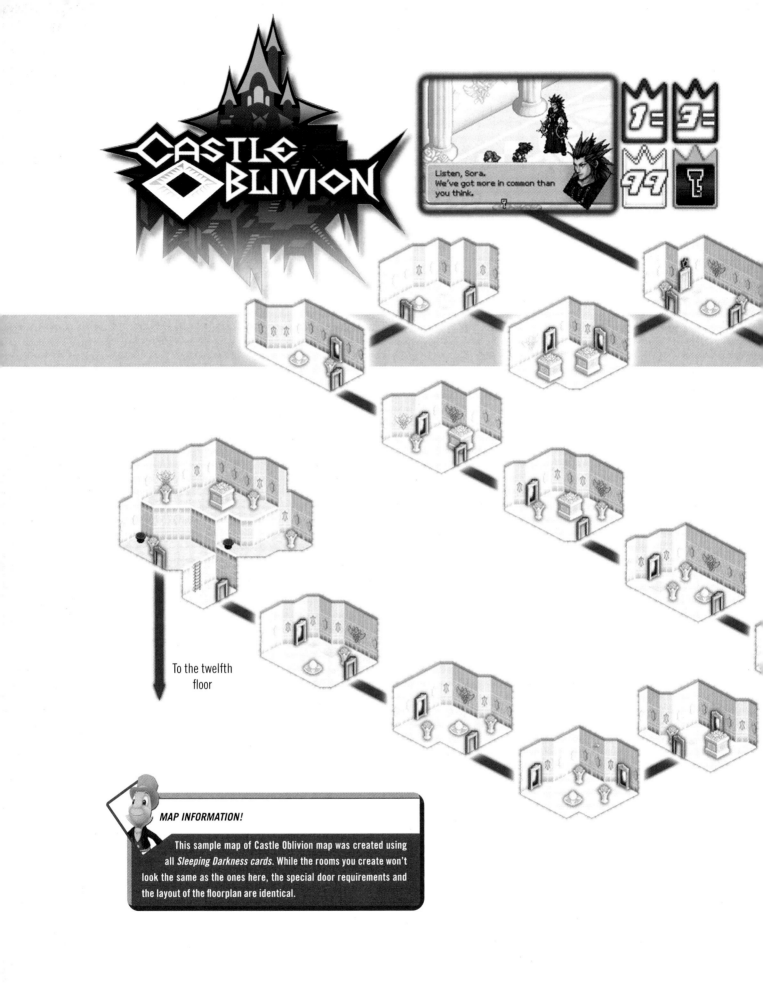

Listen, Sora.
We've got more in common than you think.

To the twelfth floor

MAP INFORMATION!

This sample map of Castle Oblivion map was created using all *Sleeping Darkness cards*. While the rooms you create won't look the same as the ones here, the special door requirements and the layout of the floorplan are identical.

Get real, Marluxia.
Let Naminé go!

MAP CARDS

Tranquil Darkness

Teeming Darkness

Feeble Darkness

Almighty Darkness

Sleeping Darkness

Looming Darkness

Calm Bounty

Guarded Trove

False Bounty

Moment's Reprieve

Moogle Room

Mingling Worlds

Key to Rewards

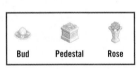

Bud   Pedestal   Rose

COMMON HEARTLESS

Axel (boss)

Blue Rhapsody

Darkball

Defender

Green Requiem

Marluxia (boss)

Neoshadow

Red Nocturne

Shadow

Wizard

Wyvern

Yellow Opera

COMMON BATTLE CARDS

Diamond Dust

Ultima Weapon

NEW SLEIGHTS

Trinity Limit

The thirteenth floor is the largest floor thus far and it's stocked with some of the most challenging Heartless. To make it through safely, give considerable thought as to where to open Moment's Reprieve rooms. Try opening two of these rooms in the positions shown on the maps (see previous section). The first room is placed at the end of the first six rooms you must open on your way to the Key of Beginnings room. This provides needed relief as you travel through the first part of the floor and it serves as a handy save point later when the room joins up with the exit room. Also, try opening a second Moment's Reprieve room off the Key of Beginnings room. This serves as another halfway point through the floor, acting as a place to save and heal before taking on Axel in the story room.

Don't expect this floor to be a walk in the park. There are many rooms to open and lots of Heartless to fight before you take on the final bosses (yes, there's more than one). Castle Oblivion introduces the final new Heartless in the game: the Neoshadow. These creatures are an upgraded version of the standard Shadow. They are fast, tough and can dodge attacks by going into "two-dimensional" mode, which makes them invulnerable to attack.

Trinity Limit is the bomb! Unfortunately, Neoshadows like to go into "two-dimensional" mode just before the attack takes effect, protecting them from the blast!

Neoshadows go into "2D" mode when threatened by a magical type of attack.

To even the score—and celebrate the return of Goofy and Donald!—Sora learns the most helpful sleight in the game at the entrance to the thirteenth floor: **Trinity Limit**. To trigger this attack, stock an attack card with a Donald and Goofy friend card and voila! This creates a powerful attack that covers the entire battlefield. It's even better than the combination of Shock Impact and Ragnarok. Trinity Limit also makes Meeting Place cards the perfect map cards for Castle Oblivion!

Since this is the final floor, the final bosses aren't far behind. Now is the time to finish collecting any cards you've missed. Take some time to revisit all of the previous 12 floors. Pick up any missed enemy cards, verify that you found all of the Key to Rewards treasures, and open at least two Calm Bounty rooms per floor just to ensure that you found all of the unique prizes. Doing this is also a good way to level up before the big fights!

You can expect longer and more difficult Heartless battles, too. Don't be afraid to escape from a battle if things get too tough. Also, there are no new friends here nor is there a Key to Rewards room to add to your treasures. Story rooms are limited to one: the Key of Beginnings room. And, the final battles take place in the hallway past the Castle Oblivion exit.

BOSS BATTLE AXEL

Fire Wall is still as deadly as ever, unless you're on the opposite side of the wall.

Card break Firetooth as soon as possible. When you see Axel's flaming hands, look for a zero card immediately. Of course, a good Dodge Roll is always a decent alternative.

The best time to attack Axel is actually when he's recharging his deck, as his defenses are down and he can't strike back.

Axel has grown much stronger in the time between the last fight. Perhaps he was holding back then, but his gloves are off now and he's prepared to fight to the death!

Axel uses fire-based abilities. Fire Wall was one of his favorite sleights during the first fight, and it's still a standby in his arsenal now.

Joining the fray is the new, powerful fireball attack called Firetooth. In this sleight, Axel flings two homing fireballs from his hands. These fireballs continue to circle Sora until you either card break them or they stop causing damage. His ability, Fire Boost, increases the damage his fire attacks inflict, so be careful when you see it flashing in the bottom-right corner of the screen.

Don't expect this battle to be easy. Axel is swift and can warp around the battlefield, making it hard to pin him down. To be successful you must continuously card break his attacks while connecting with multiple hits. Curaga combos are ultimately your best bet on the health front.

DECK STRATEGIES

Take the deck that you used against the Riku replica in the hallway between the twelfth and thirteenth floors and go through it with a fine-toothed comb. If you can, make sure your entire deck is comprised of zeros and 9s. If you have a large inventory of cards, make sure that you upgrade your attack cards, choosing more powerful Keyblades over the more common, but less powerful, ones. This will make a big difference in the upcoming battles. Lastly, take along about six Cure cards and a high-numbered (8 or 9) Megalixir or Potion/Hi-Potion at the end.

INSIDE THE BOSS'S DECK

Axel may be more dangerous than before but he's only added a single sleight to his repertoire. The rest is all the same. Firetooth, the new sleight, is made up of an "A" card, a "B" card and another "A" card.

His deck is as follows:
"A" attack cards: 0 (x3); 1 (x2); 2 (x2); 3 (x2); 4 (x3); 5 (x3); 6 (x3); 7 (x2); 8 (x3); 9 (x3)
"B" attack cards: 0 (x3); 1 (x3); 2 (x2); 3 (x3); 4 (x3); 5 (x3); 6 (x2); 7 (x3); 8 (x2); 9 (x3)
Elixir: 0 (x1); 9 (x1)
Enemy cards: Axel, Red Nocturne

INTO THE CASTLE HALLS: THE FINAL FIGHT

After the fight with Axel, it's time to head into the hallway beyond the thirteenth floor. This is where you fight Marluxia. This battle is conducted in two stages. First, the fight involves just Marluxia. Then, you have to defeat him a second time as he rides in a well-armored mech. Win both bouts to defeat the game.

BOSS BATTLE MARLUXIA

Marluxia prepares to slice Sora with one of his dramatic scythe sweeps!

The Deathscythe swoops down on Sora. Because of Double Sleight, you get to go through this twice unless you card break the attack.

Marluxia is an enigmatic foe. You'd expect him to be extremely difficult (his attacks are really impressive looking), but he doesn't seem to inflict the kind of damage that you'd expect. Marluxia's weapon of choice is the scythe. This weapon gives him longer than average reach and extends his normal attack range from simple strokes to dramatic slashes.

In addition, Marluxia has access to two big sleights: Deathscythe and Blossom Shower, both of which are boosted by his Double Sleight ability.

The first, Deathscythe, summons a giant scythe to slice Sora. It's big and scary, but doesn't inflict a lot of damage. However, the sight of it is enough to make you select the nearest zero card to card break the attack.

His second big attack, Blossom Shower, rains a swirl of sharp petals down on the battlefield. Again, the intro to this attack is impressive enough to make you start searching for a zero card to interrupt its progress.

To do well in this fight, use zero cards to break Marluxia's big attacks and use level 9 cards to pound on him as often and as long as possible. Heal at the end of every card round, even if Sora isn't hurting that much. Sleights are fine, but they don't inflict as much damage as regular weapon cards. Besides, Marluxia has

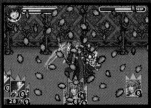

Blossom Shower in all its glory.

Trinity Limit seems like it would be a great attack against Marluxia, yet it doesn't inflict very much damage.

his own reserve of zero cards and isn't afraid to use them!

At the end of this battle, return to the closest save point and prepare for the final battle against Marluxia.

INSIDE THE BOSS'S DECK

Marluxia's first form has plenty of attacks. Three of them are tied to his three attack cards. To the red "A" and "C" cards, the attacks crescent shockwave and phantom cyber are attached. A circular rejection is the attack spawned from his blue "B" card. Marluxia also has two sleights. Blossom Shower is comprised of a "B" card + an "A" card + a "B" card, while Deathscythe requires an "A", "B", and "C" card.

His deck is as follows:
"A" attack cards: 0 (x2);
1 (x1); 2 (x1); 3 (x1); 4 (x2);
5 (x2); 6 (x2); 7 (x3); 8 (x3);
9 (x3)
"B" attack cards: 0 (x2);
1 (x1); 2 (x1); 3 (x1); 4 (x2);
5 (x2); 6 (x2); 7 (x3); 8 (x3);
9 (x3)
"C" attack cards: 0 (x2);
1 (x1); 2 (x1); 3 (x1); 4 (x2);
5 (x2); 6 (x2); 7 (x3); 8 (x3);
9 (x3)
Elixir: 9 (x2)
Enemy card: Marluxia

The final battle begins!

Don't worry about the petals floating above. Concentrate on taking out the two sword appendages first.

The final battle pits Sora against the "real" Marluxia in a mech suit. Again, this battle is quite manageable if you can block the big attacks, keep Sora's HP gauge(s) full, and connect with plenty of attacks.

This battle takes a while to play through. First, destroy the two swords on the end of the mech. This is somewhat easy to accomplish, because Marluxia doesn't do much to prevent it from happening. At the most, he'll cast one of his petal bullet spells, but the damage they cause is minimal and you can card break it easily.

The auto-targeting locks onto the petals floating around Marluxia when he's not available for pummeling. However, there are times when Marluxia uses this tendency to detract attention from himself. If you think that you can attack Marluxia, change your position or angle of attack to see if the target changes to him. Use the target as your guide.

There's no need to suffer from this attack when you can card break it before it even happens.

After you destroy the two swords on the mech, it's time to start working on Marluxia. There are certain points at which Marluxia is vulnerable to attack. Look for the targeting icon to attach itself to Marluxia's chest and start swinging.

Marluxia may attempt to skewer Sora with the underside of the mech unit. When you see him jump with the vehicle, immediately card break the impending attack. In truth, this is little more than a shock wave attack, but the damage it inflicts can be impressive. Besides, it is fairly easy to break.

After the jump attack, the battle can go in many directions. Basically, whenever Marluxia is open to attack, head over to him and pound away with Sora's Keyblade. Ignore the frequent bursts of flower petals and concentrate on taking down Marluxia.

Once you empty Marluxia's HP Gauge (he has *four* of them!), sit back and watch as the story is resolved. Feel proud, for you have fought long and hard for this!

If only all parts of the battle were this easy.

When this occurs, focus on the petals flying overhead until Marluxia comes out from his flowery cocoon. Then you can attack him, at least until the wind drags Sora away and off the mech.

Watch out when Marluxia summons these glowing pink orbs. Once the spell is cast, they home in on Sora and cut right through him. This attack usually occurs after jump attacks and almost always when you're trying to reload your deck!

Marluxia may even hit Sora with his ship. You can card break this like the jump attack, but the uncertainty of when he'll strike makes the timing more difficult.

SECRETS OF THE GAME

After clearing the final battle in the main game, a new mode opens after the credits roll called called Reverse/Rebirth. This mode unlocks two new options on the Start Menu: **Link Mode** and **Riku Mode**.

RIKU MODE

Riku Mode enables you to play the game from Riku's perspective. It seems that while Sora and his pals were working their way up to the top of Castle Oblivion looking for Riku and King Mickey, Riku was trying to make his way up from the castle's basement levels, facing many of the same foes that Sora faced. Does Riku manage to seal off the darkness within him? Will the two friends meet up and reconcile at the end? You'll have to play through to find out!

Completing the game as Sora causes the opening screen to change to the Reverse/Rebirth graphic.

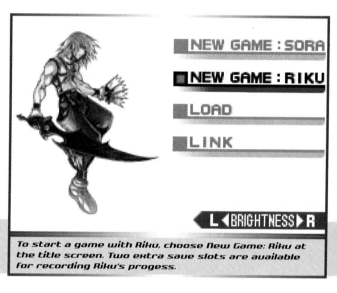

To start a game with Riku, choose New Game: Riku at the title screen. Two extra save slots are available for recording Riku's progess.

DIFFERENCES BETWEEN THE RIKU GAME AND THE SORA GAME

On one hand, playing as Riku is quite similar to playing as Sora. Each character's objectives are identical: Clear each floor by defeating the main boss and make it to the top floor and, hopefully, resolution and escape. Of course, how each character gets there is what distinguishes the two modes.

Ultimately, the Riku game is a streamlined version of the Sora game. There is only one story room per floor and fewer boss fights overall. Riku visits all of the same worlds as Sora (with the exception of the Hundred Acre Wood), but the order in which he visits them is different.

The major difference between the two modes, however, is in the cards that Riku uses. As you'll soon discover, the first time you try to reorganize your card deck, Riku's deck is considered a *closed* deck. In other words, the deck is predetermined and may not be altered. Your job is to determine how to maximize the deck you are given.

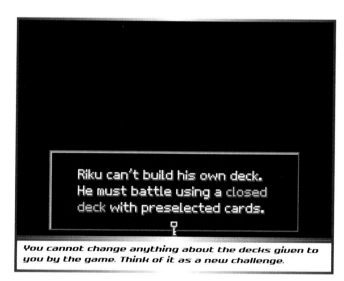

You cannot change anything about the decks given to you by the game. Think of it as a new challenge.

THE CLOSED DECK SYSTEM

The good thing about the closed deck system is that it alleviates the hassle of hunting down new cards, conserving Moogle Points, and micro-managing your deck. Instead, it enables you to concentrate more on the mechanics and strategy of the game. Of course, if you enjoyed hunting down new cards and micro-managing your deck, then you may feel that something is missing from the new game.

Riku's card deck changes with each world you visit. The only variables are the enemy cards. After you defeat a boss, his or her enemy card is added to your deck and remains there, regardless of the order you decide to visit the different worlds. Since you know the bosses and you've seen their respective enemy cards, you should be able to apply strategy to the order in which you visit each world.

The enemy cards in your deck change depending upon the bosses you've previously fought. For example, the Traverse Town decks shown above differ based on previously opened worlds. The first screen shows the deck when you open Traverse Town on Basement Eleven and the second deck shows the deck when you open that world on Basement Eight, after defeating Jafar, Parasite Cage, and Captain Hook.

The decks used in Riku Mode are largely comprised of attack cards. Riku has one weapon, the Soul Eater, and all decks are based around that card. To boost the weapon's power, consider raising his Attack Power when he levels up. At the start of the game, most decks have at least one item card like Potion or Hi-Potion, but they disappear the further you advance in the game. No magic cards are used in Riku's decks, so if you relied on magic a lot as you played through the Sora game, it may take a while to get used to playing with only attack cards.

On the other hand, Riku's closed decks should inspire you to start including enemy cards during your battles. These cards can be easily overlooked in the Sora game, but they can be a lifesaver when playing as Riku. Of course, Riku has other powers that make magic unnecessary...

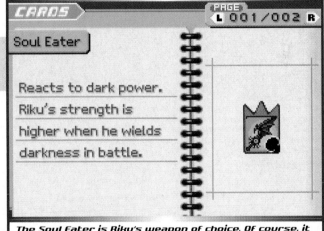

The Soul Eater is Riku's weapon of choice. Of course, it helps that he has no other choice in weapons.

WELCOME TO
CASTLE OBLIVION

CHARACTERS

GAME BASICS

CASTLE OBLIVION

SECRETS OF
THE GAME

THE CARDS

BESTIARY

DARK MODE

Ansem switches on Dark Mode. This mode increases Riku's strength, giving him an advantage over most enemies.

After defeating the boss on Basement Twelve, Hollow Bastion, you are confronted by Riku's nemesis, Ansem. Defeat him to learn how to use Riku's latent darkness in battle. It's called "Dark Mode" and it enables Riku, under certain circumstances, to transform into Dark Riku. Dark Riku is identical in power to the Riku replica you fought as Sora. When Riku is in Dark Mode, his strength increases, his speed decreases, and he can perform sleights.

Riku knows three sleights: **Dark Break**, **Dark Firaga**, and **Dark Aura**. Dark Firaga and Dark Aura should be very familiar, but Dark Break is a new one. In addition, Riku can also attack while jumping, causing him to perform his jump and slash combo. Pressing the B Button while he's in the air enables him to land behind the targeted enemy.

Dark Break enables Riku to leap into the air and pound on enemies from the air. It requires three Soul Eater cards whose total value falls between 5 and 15. This is a great attack that has a decent duration and it enables Riku to switch targets once he's pounded an enemy to death.

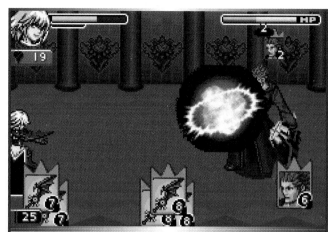

Dark Firaga is Riku's fireball of dark energy. This sleight was a standby of the Riku replica in Sora's story, so it should be familiar. It requires three Soul Eater cards whose total value lies between 16 and 25.

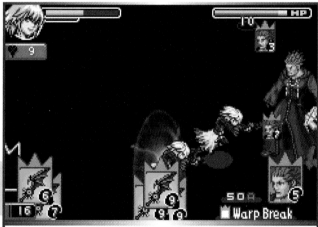

Remember the days when Dark Aura used to be your worst nightmare in a battle with Riku? Now you can use it to terrorize other creatures! Dark Aura requires three Soul Eater cards with a total value of 27. In other words, you need three 9s to pull it off!

Watch for the number that appears when you perform a card break. The more points you get, the quicker you can enter Dark Mode.

Riku enters Dark Mode whenever his Dark Points (DP) gauge fills up. Card breaking your foe's cards or taking damage is key to filling up the gauge. In battle, when you card break an opponent, you'll notice a number next to the Card Break exclamation. This is the difference in value between the two cards and it is added to your Dark Points.

After Riku's Dark Points reach a certain level, he turns into Dark Riku. Riku stays in Dark Mode until his DP runs out through damage from enemies or when you lose a card break.

In Dark Mode, Riku's costume changes to that of the Riku replica.

OTHER DIFFERENCES

There are a few more small differences between Sora Mode and Riku Mode that you need to know about. The best difference is the fact that you no longer have to wait to reload your deck. Riku's deck reloads instantly when you press the A Button after selecting the reload card, or when you run out of cards completely.

Another difference revolves around friends. Riku can summon only one friend, but he's worth almost all of Sora's friends combined: King Mickey! The King card (separate from the trick cards with the Mickey Mouse logo picked up in boss battles) summons King Mickey to the battlefield where he restores HP, stuns and inflicts damage on all enemies, and reloads your cards. When you stock two or three the King cards as a combo (you can do this in or out of Dark Mode), King Mickey arrives and inflicts extra damage and extra healing. In boss fights, these cards can be a lifesaver—literally!

Summoning King Mickey is always a smart thing to do in battle.

And speaking of cards, Riku has access to fewer map cards than Sora. When you are creating rooms, use the bonuses these rooms provide to your advantage. Keep in mind that the Mingling Worlds card can only draw from the other rooms listed when randomly creating a world! The map cards in Riku Mode are as follows:

Tranquil Darkness	Sleeping Darkness	Meeting Ground	Moment's Reprieve
Teeming Darkness	Looming Darkness	Stagnant Space	Mingling Worlds
Feeble Darkness	Martial Waking	Strong Initiative	
Almighty Darkness	Alchemic Waking	Lasting Daze	

WELCOME TO CASTLE OBLIVION

CHARACTERS

GAME BASICS

CASTLE OBLIVION

SECRETS OF THE GAME

THE CARDS

BESTIARY

Riku can also jump higher than Sora, which enables him to jump on top of Treasure Spots that Sora has to jump down on to trigger, like the three Treasure Spots in Halloween Town. Of course, it doesn't matter as much in Riku Mode, because Treasure Spots only release HP prizes.

When Riku levels up, he has the opportunity to increase three stats: his Hit Points, Attack Power, and his Dark Points. Attack Boost appears every five levels and raises Riku's AP by 1 point. HP Boost raises Riku's HP by 15 points and Darkness Boost increases Riku's DP by 2 points. Riku's HP maxes out at 560 points, while his AP maxes out at 30 and his DP at 100.

Riku can jump almost twice as high as Sora, allowing him to reach the tops of taller platforms and certain Treasure Spots more easily.

When Riku levels up, you have the choice to increase one of three stats. These are different than Sora's choices, because of the changes to the game.

In summary, the differences between the Riku game and the Sora game are as follows:

- Usually, there are no events in individual worlds. Story-related events take place in the castle halls.
- Riku's deck of cards for each floor is *fixed* and cannot be altered in any way.
- When Riku levels up, you can allocate points to his Hit Points, Attack Power or Dark Points.
- There are no premium prizes or Moogle Shops.
- Riku has access to fewer map cards than Sora.
- Treasure Spots only produce HP prizes when triggered.
- Riku can jump higher than Sora.
- Riku is faster than Sora but, as a result, tends to slide when stopping.
- Instead of a Dodge Roll, Riku performs a back step when you tap twice on the D-Pad in a single direction.
- In battle, Riku's deck has an auto-reload feature when he runs out of battle cards.
- Riku can only perform sleights when he is in Dark Mode.

RIKU

Sora's childhood friend. Baited by the darkness and used by Maleficent and Ansem, Riku once fought against Sora. In order to seal the door to darkness, Riku stayed with the king on the other side. His current whereabouts are unknown. Sora journeys in the hopes of finding Riku.

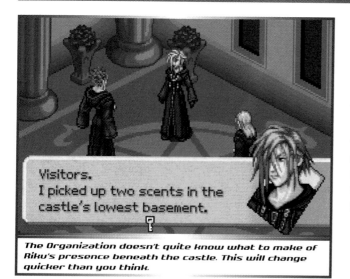

Visitors.
I picked up two scents in the castle's lowest basement.

The Organization doesn't quite know what to make of Riku's presence beneath the castle. This will change quicker than you think.

Riku starts his journey on Basement Twelve. He must travel to Basement One through the same worlds that Sora visited, minus the Hundred Acre Wood. Along the way, prepare to meet members of the Organization, both old and new.

The main difference between the Riku game and the Sora game after Basement Twelve is that the ultimate goal in each world is to defeat the boss. Riku gets to bypass all of the story rooms from Sora Mode and only fights the main boss. This, however, presents you with an interesting dilemma: Do you clear each room of all their Heartless on the way to the single boss room on each floor, or do you proceed straight to the boss room, forgoing the opportunity to level up?

Compare the Monstro map in Sora's game to that in the Riku game.

There are advantages to doing both. On one hand, the world bosses are, on the whole, somewhat easy to defeat with the decks provided. This is largely because you should be familiar with their attacks and weaknesses from fighting them in the Sora game. However, the Organization bosses you meet in the hallway are largely new and can be quite difficult to subdue. If you get stuck in a battle, return to the previous world and level up a bit. Increasing Riku's AP or adding to his HP or Dark Points (DP) can help you retain your edge in battle. Also, don't underestimate the importance of enemy cards for a good defense. Riku's Dark Mode is also key to victory in many battles, as it increases Riku's strength and enables him to use killer sleights like Dark Aura. Oftentimes, all you need to do to defeat a tough boss is unleash a couple of Dark Aura attacks!

OUTLINE OF EVENTS

The following is a skeletal outline of the main events that occur in the Riku game. Use this as a point of reference while playing through the game so that you know what's coming up next. This will enable you to prepare for important fights with members of the Organization or other special bosses.

BASEMENT TWELVE: HOLLOW BASTION

Main Events

1. Visit all three story rooms. Defeat the boss, Dragon Maleficent.

2. Fight Ansem in the castle hall. Acquire the ability to use Dark Mode and get The King friend card. Obtain four world cards.

BASEMENT ELEVEN TO BASEMENT EIGHT

Main Events

1. The following world cards are available at this time: Agrabah, Monstro, Never Land, and Traverse Town. Defeat the main boss for each world (Jafar, Parasite Cage, Captain Hook, and Guard Armor) to progress to the next floor.

2. Battle against Vexen in the Hallway between Basement Ten and Basement Nine.

3. Fight against the Riku replica (Battle #1) in the Hallway between Basement Eight and Basement Seven.

4. Obtain four new world cards from Ansem in the Hallway between Basement Eight and Basement Seven.

BASEMENT SEVEN TO BASEMENT FOUR

Main Events

1. The following world cards are available at this time: Atlantica, Olympus Coliseum, Wonderland, and Halloween Town. Defeat the main boss for each world (Ursula, Hades, Trickmaster, and Oogie Boogie) to progress to the next floor.

2. Battle against Lexaeus.

BASEMENT THREE: DESTINY ISLANDS

Main Events

1. King Mickey doesn't join Riku in this world (i.e., no The King card).

2. Defeat the boss, Darkside.

BASEMENT TWO: TWILIGHT TOWN

Main Events

1. King Mickey doesn't join Riku in this world (i.e., no The King card).

2. Defeat the boss, the Riku replica (Battle #2).

BASEMENT ONE: CASTLE OBLIVION

Main Events

1. Defeat final boss, Ansem

2. End of game.

BOSS STRATEGIES

This section provides some basic tips and strategies for fighting the *new* bosses in Riku Mode. It does not include information on enemies you've already fought as Sora, since the information about them hasn't changed. It's up to you to determine how to use the decks provided to take out these old foes.

BOSS BATTLE ANSEM (BATTLE #1)

Location: Hallway Between Basement Twelve and Basement Eleven

This battle is fairly straightforward. You have a good deck on your side and it's early enough in the game that Ansem isn't going to throw anything outrageously tough at Riku. Watch out for his shadow, as it has its own attacks if you dare to get too close. Just remember the basics of card battle and you'll defeat Ansem with plenty of HP to spare.

INSIDE THE BOSS'S DECK

In this battle, Ansem has two cards, red and blue, that are keyed to his two basic attacks. The blue "A" card controls his dark claw attack, while the red "B" card triggers his shockwave attack. Ansem has a single sleight at this point that is made by combining one "A" card and two "B" cards.

His deck is as follows:

"A" attack cards: 0 (x1); 1 (x1); 2 (x1); 3 (x1); 4 (x1); 5 (x1); 6 (x1); 7 (x1); 8 (x1); 9 (x1)

"B" attack cards: 0 (x1); 1 (x1); 2 (x1); 3 (x1); 4 (x1); 5 (x1); 6 (x1); 7 (x1); 8 (x1); 9 (x1)

No enemy or item cards.

WELCOME TO CASTLE OBLIVION

CHARACTERS

GAME BASICS

CASTLE OBLIVION

SECRETS OF THE GAME

THE CARDS

BESTIARY

BOSS BATTLE VEXEN

Location: Hallway between Basement Ten and Basement Nine

Vexen's invulnerability to frontal attacks makes this boss tough—especially if you are still trying to make Riku perform a Dodge Roll! Instead when you are in Dark Mode, target Vexen, jump into the air and press B to land behind him. Vexen enters this battle with a new sleight, Diamond Dust. Although rarely used, this new attack is quite spectacular. To defeat Vexen, keep out of the way of Vexen's Freeze attack, keep up your health, and don't lose patience as you chip away at his HP.

INSIDE THE BOSS'S DECK

As in the Sora game, Vexen's two normal attacks are keyed to two attack cards. The blue "A" card triggers his Blizzara attack and the red "B" card holds his shield attack. The new sleight, Diamond Dust, is a Riku Mode exclusive and takes a "B" card and two "A" cards to perform.

His deck is as follows:

"A" attack cards: 0 (x3); 1 (x2); 2 (x1); 7 (x1); 8 (x2); 9 (x3)

"B" attack cards: 0 (x3); 1 (x2); 2 (x1); 7 (x1); 8 (x2); 9 (x3)

Mega-Elixir: 4 (x1); 5 (x1)

Elixir: 0 (x1); 1 (x1); 8 (x1); 9 (x1)

Enemy card: Vexen, Blue Rhapsody, Air Pirate

BOSS BATTLE RIKU REPLICA (BATTLE #1)

Location: Hallway between Basement Eight and Basement Seven

It feels sort of strange to be fighting Riku (or the Riku replica) *as* Riku. At this point, you should have a good handle on Riku's strengths and weaknesses, so try to exploit Riku replica's weaknesses. As with most boss fights, getting into Dark Mode quickly is the key to victory. Dark Mode sleights cause lots of damage and can drain multiple HP gauges much quicker than standard physical attacks.

I bet it's not every day you meet your twin.

INSIDE THE BOSS'S DECK

This deck is very similar to the deck used in the second Riku replica fight in the Sora game. He has three attack cards for three attacks and the sleight Dark Firaga is made by combining two "A" cards and a "C".

His deck is as follows:

"A" attack cards: 0 (x2); 1 (x1); 2 (x2); 3 (x2); 4 (x3); 5 (x3); 6 (x2); 7 (x2); 8 (x1); 9 (x2)

"B" attack cards: 0 (x2); 2 (x1); 3 (x1); 4 (x1); 5 (x1); 6 (x1); 7 (x1); 9 (x2)

"C" attack cards: 1 (x2); 4 (x2); 5 (x3); 6 (x2); 8 (x2)

Elixir: 4 (x1); 5 (x1); 6 (x1)

Enemy card: Shadow

BOSS BATTLE LEXAEUS

Location: Hallway between Basement Four and Basement Three

Lexaeus uses earth magic, something you haven't seen yet in the game. Attacks like Rockshatter can take you by surprise if you aren't prepared. In general, though, this shouldn't be a very difficult fight. As always, use Dark Mode to your advantage!

INSIDE THE BOSS'S DECK

Lexaeus has three attack cards for his three attacks. The red "A" and "B" cards control his combination and tomahawk attacks, while the blue "B" card triggers his shockwave style quake attack. His sleight, Rockshatter, is created by combining an "A" card + "B" card + "A" card.

His deck is as follows:

"A" attack cards: 0 (x2); 1 (x2); 2 (x2); 3 (x2); 4 (x2); 5 (x2); 6 (x2); 7 (x2); 8 (x2); 9 (x2)

"B" attack cards: 3 (x3); 4 (x3); 5 (x3); 6 (x3); 7 (x3); 8 (x3)

"C" attack cards: 0 (x1); 1 (x1); 2 (x1); 3 (x1); 4 (x1); 5 (x1); 6 (x1); 7 (x1); 8 (x1); 9 (x1)

Enemy card: Lexaeus

BOSS BATTLE RIKU REPLICA (BATTLE #2)

Location: Basement Two, Twilight Town

This is the toughest battle in Riku Mode. The Riku replica is just as tough and fast as he was when you fought him at the end of the Sora game. To make this fight even tougher, you must use the average Twilight Town deck and fight without the aid of King Mickey. In other words, you have to win without any form of healing! It's tough, but not impossible. Your best chance of survival is to get to Dark Mode as soon as possible and hope that you have enough DP to stay there until the end of the battle. The Riku replica uses Dark Aura a lot and you don't have the zero cards to break the attack every time. Instead, use combos to card break his attacks and try to land as many of the Dark Mode sleights as possible. A few Dark Break attacks are enough to get his HP down significantly!

INSIDE THE BOSS'S DECK

This deck is very similar to the deck used in the fourth battle against the Riku replica in the Sora game. He has four attacks and two sleights, including the devastating Dark Aura attack.

His deck is as follows:

"A" attack cards: 0 (x2); 1 (x2); 3 (x2); 4 (x3); 5 (x3); 6 (x2); 8 (x2); 9 (x2)

"B" attack cards: 0 (x2); 1 (x2); 2 (x1); 3 (x2); 4 (x3); 5 (x3); 6 (x2); 7 (x1); 8 (x2); 9 (x2)

"C" attack cards: 1 (x1); 2 (x1); 3 (x1); 4 (x2); 5 (x2); 6 (x2); 7 (x1); 8 (x1)

"D" attack cards: 0 (x1); 1 (x2); 2 (x2); 7 (x2); 8 (x2); 9 (x1)

Elixir: 4 (x1); 5 (x2); 6 (x1); 9 (x1)

Enemy cards: Riku, Shadow

WELCOME TO CASTLE OBLIVION

CHARACTERS

GAME BASICS

CASTLE OBLIVION

SECRETS OF THE GAME

THE CARDS

BESTIARY

BOSS BATTLE ANSEM (BATTLE #2)

Location: Basement One, Castle Oblivion

If you don't want any strategy on how to defeat the final boss in Riku Mode, then stop reading now! Try to win the fight on your own first, then refer back to this section for some tips and strategy.

Basically, you are fighting a more powerful version of the Ansem you battled at the start of the game. He is guarded—literally—by his dark shadow, making it very hard to land even standard physical attacks. Instead, try to make it to Dark Mode as fast as possible so that you can hit him with Dark Aura attacks or even Dark Breaks. Collect the King cards and stock them to provide max healing when you need it. This battle isn't extremely difficult, especially compared to the Riku replica boss fight in Twilight Town.

INSIDE THE BOSS'S DECK

This time around, Ansem's deck is fully beefed up for battle. The newest addition to his arsenal is the sleight, Dark Shadow, which is created by combining an "A" card + "B" card + "A" card.

His deck is as follows:

"A" attack cards: 0 (x5); 1 (x4); 2 (x4); 3 (x4); 4 (x4); 5 (x4); 6 (x4); 7 (x4); 8 (x4); 9 (x5)

"B" attack cards: 0 (x5); 1 (x4); 2 (x4); 3 (x4); 4 (x4); 5 (x4); 6 (x4); 7 (x4); 8 (x4); 9 (x5)

Elixir: 9 (x2)

Enemy card: Ansem

A LIST OF DECKS BY WORLD

The following is a list of all the card decks per world. Use these to help plan out boss strategies and other tactics before entering a particular story room. These lists do *not* include boss enemy cards. Your deck will include the enemy cards of all bosses defeated up to the point at which you enter a specific world.

HALLOW BASTION

Soul Eater 9	Soul Eater 6	Soul Eater 5	Potion 9
Soul Eater 8	Soul Eater 7	Soul Eater 4	Defender
Soul Eater 7	Soul Eater 6	Soul Eater 5	
Soul Eater 8	Soul Eater 5	Soul Eater 4	
Soul Eater 7	Soul Eater 6	Soul Eater 3	

Soul Eater 8	Soul Eater 6	Soul Eater 8	Hi-Potion 9
Soul Eater 8	Soul Eater 9	Soul Eater 6	Hi-Potion 0
Soul Eater 8	Soul Eater 9	Soul Eater 7	Soul Eater 0
Soul Eater 7	Soul Eater 9	Soul Eater 9	Soul Eater 0
Soul Eater 7	Soul Eater 6	Soul Eater 9	Soul Eater 0
Soul Eater 7	Soul Eater 7	Soul Eater 6	Soul Eater 0
Soul Eater 6	Soul Eater 8	Soul Eater 7	
Soul Eater 6	Soul Eater 9	Soul Eater 8	

AGRABAH

Soul Eater 7	Soul Eater 4	Soul Eater 7	Soul Eater 4
Soul Eater 6	Soul Eater 3	Soul Eater 6	Soul Eater 3
Soul Eater 4	Soul Eater 7	Soul Eater 4	Hi-Potion 7
Soul Eater 3	Soul Eater 6	Soul Eater 3	Fat Bandit
Soul Eater 7	Soul Eater 4	Soul Eater 7	
Soul Eater 6	Soul Eater 3	Soul Eater 6	

MONSTRO

Soul Eater 7	Soul Eater 4	Soul Eater 7	Soul Eater 4
Soul Eater 5	Soul Eater 1	Soul Eater 6	Soul Eater 1
Soul Eater 4	Soul Eater 7	Soul Eater 4	Search Ghost
Soul Eater 1	Soul Eater 6	Soul Eater 1	
Soul Eater 7	Soul Eater 4	Soul Eater 7	
Soul Eater 5	Soul Eater 1	Soul Eater 6	

NEVER LAND

Soul Eater 7	Soul Eater 2	Soul Eater 2	Soul Eater 7
Soul Eater 6	Soul Eater 4	Soul Eater 3	Soul Eater 8
Soul Eater 5	Soul Eater 1	Soul Eater 4	Soul Eater 9
Soul Eater 4	Soul Eater 0	Soul Eater 5	Pirate
Soul Eater 3	Soul Eater 1	Soul Eater 6	

TRAVERSE TOWN

Soul Eater 4	Soul Eater 7
Soul Eater 5	Soul Eater 8
Soul Eater 6	Shadow

ATLANTICA

Soul Eater 5	Soul Eater 4	Soul Eater 2	Soul Eater 1
Soul Eater 5	Soul Eater 4	Soul Eater 2	Soul Eater 1
Soul Eater 5	Soul Eater 3	Soul Eater 2	Sea Neon
Soul Eater 5	Soul Eater 3	Soul Eater 2	
Soul Eater 4	Soul Eater 3	Soul Eater 1	
Soul Eater 4	Soul Eater 3	Soul Eater 1	

OLYMPUS COLISEUM

Soul Eater 1	Soul Eater 7	Soul Eater 1	Soul Eater 0
Soul Eater 2	Soul Eater 8	Soul Eater 1	Soul Eater 0
Soul Eater 3	Soul Eater 9	Soul Eater 1	Soul Eater 0
Soul Eater 4	Soul Eater 1	Soul Eater 1	Powerwild
Soul Eater 5	Soul Eater 1	Soul Eater 1	
Soul Eater 6	Soul Eater 1	Soul Eater 1	

WONDERLAND

Soul Eater 3	Soul Eater 4	Soul Eater 5	Large Body
Soul Eater 4	Soul Eater 5	Soul Eater 3	
Soul Eater 5	Soul Eater 3	Soul Eater 4	
Soul Eater 3	Soul Eater 4	Soul Eater 5	

HALLOWEEN TOWN

Soul Eater 7	Soul Eater 4	Soul Eater 7	Soul Eater 4
Soul Eater 7	Soul Eater 4	Soul Eater 7	Wight Knight
Soul Eater 6	Soul Eater 5	Soul Eater 7	
Soul Eater 6	Soul Eater 5	Soul Eater 6	
Soul Eater 5	Soul Eater 6	Soul Eater 5	
Soul Eater 5	Soul Eater 6	Soul Eater 6	

DESTINY ISLANDS

Soul Eater 0	Soul Eater 0	Soul Eater 6	Soul Eater 5
Soul Eater 1	Soul Eater 2	Soul Eater 4	Soul Eater 3
Soul Eater 3	Soul Eater 4	Soul Eater 2	Soul Eater 2
Soul Eater 5	Soul Eater 6	Soul Eater 0	Soul Eater 0
Soul Eater 7	Soul Eater 8	Soul Eater 7	

Soul Eater 9	Soul Eater 4	Soul Eater 5	Soul Eater 8
Soul Eater 6	Soul Eater 1	Soul Eater 3	Soul Eater 0
Soul Eater 3	Soul Eater 6	Soul Eater 1	Soul Eater 2
Soul Eater 8	Soul Eater 3	Soul Eater 0	Soul Eater 9
Soul Eater 5	Soul Eater 0	Soul Eater 2	
Soul Eater 2	Soul Eater 9	Soul Eater 4	
Soul Eater 7	Soul Eater 7	Soul Eater 6	

CASTLE OBLIVION

Soul Eater 8	Soul Eater 6	Soul Eater 8	Hi-Potion 9
Soul Eater 8	Soul Eater 9	Soul Eater 6	Hi-Potion 0
Soul Eater 8	Soul Eater 9	Soul Eater 7	Soul Eater 0
Soul Eater 7	Soul Eater 9	Soul Eater 9	Soul Eater 0
Soul Eater 7	Soul Eater 6	Soul Eater 9	Soul Eater 0
Soul Eater 7	Soul Eater 7	Soul Eater 6	Soul Eater 0
Soul Eater 6	Soul Eater 8	Soul Eater 7	
Soul Eater 6	Soul Eater 9	Soul Eater 8	

WELCOME TO
CASTLE OBLIVION

CHARACTERS

GAME BASICS

CASTLE OBLIVION

SECRETS OF
THE GAME

THE CARDS

BESTIARY

LINK MODE

If you've ever wondered whether or not your battle tactics would stand up to your friend's, Link Mode is the place to try them out!

Basically, Link Mode allows you to load your current Sora save and pit your Sora (and consequently any of your decks of cards) against a friend. This mode only appears once you finish Sora's story, at the same time as the Reverse/Rebirth mode opens up.

To start a link battle, connect your GBA to your friend's using a Link Cable. You both need to have your *Kingdom Hearts: Chain of Memories* cartridges inserted in your respective GBA and both of you need to have completed the Sora game and opened up Reverse/Rebirth mode.

Choose the Link option at the title screen and select Load on the following screen. This allows you to load from one of the two Sora save slots. You cannot fight a link battle with a Riku game save. Once you've loaded the game save you want to use, select Versus Battle when prompted and press the A button to establish a link.

Once the GBA's have connected with one another, you can choose the deck you want to use in the battle, set a handicap and change the location of the battlefield. When all of the options have been set to your liking, it's time to start the battle!

Battles in Link Mode are fought identically to their counterparts in the main game itself. The only difference is that your opponent appears as a shadow. His or her cards, however, are displayed in the lower right-hand corner of the screen—unless he or she has played the Darkball enemy card and activated Cardblind!

The strategies used in link battles are similar to those used in the main game, except now you are fighting against a human mind instead of computer controlled AI. If you've never really experimented with enemy cards before, take a look at what they can do when used in battle. Some of them even have special powers especially for link battles.

THE CARDS

Perhaps the most important part of *Kingdom Hearts: Chain of Memories* is the quest to get all of the game's cards. This is a relatively painless task if you remember to open at least one Calm Bounty-type room on each floor and go back to open each Key to Rewards room on every floor from the first floor to the twelfth floor once you start getting Key to Rewards cards. To find the last five cards, simply clear the Sora game (for the **Diamond Dust** and **One-Winged Angel** attack cards) and the Riku game (for the **Ultima Weapon** attack card and the **Lexaeus** and **Ansem** enemy cards).

BATTLE CARDS

There are four types of battle cards: attack cards, magic cards, item cards, and friend cards. Within the magic card category there are basic magic cards and summon cards. Summon cards enable you to call a friend into battle much like friend cards. However, they are distinguished from friend cards by the fact that you can actually collect the physical card and use them in decks. Friend cards are only available while you are fighting a battle and the ones you get depend on whether or not you have friends in that world.

ATTACK CARDS

The attack card category contains all of the Keyblades Sora collects and uses in the game. If you played the original *Kingdom Hearts* game, then most of the names should sound familiar. Different Keyblades have different strengths, so weigh the pros and cons of each type of card when determining which ones to place in your deck.

THREE WISHES

LOCATION	Agrabah, random Treasure Spots.
COMBOS	Ars Arcanum, Blitz, Blizzard Raid, Firaga Break, Fire Raid, Gravity Raid, Idyll Romp, Judgment, Omnislash, Ragnarok, Reflect Raid, Shock Impact, Sliding Dash, Sonic Blade, Stop Raid, Strike Raid, Stun Impact, Thunder Raid, Trinity Limit, Zantetsuken

STATS		DESCRIPTION
Strike	C+	Agrabah-exclusive Keyblade that is fairly strong with a fast swing and great CP requirements.
Thrust	D+	
Combo Finish	B	
Swing Speed	A	
Element	PHYSICAL	
Break Recovery	B	
Required CP	A	

KINGDOM KEY

LOCATION	Default Keyblade.
COMBOS	Ars Arcanum, Blitz, Blizzard Raid, Firaga Break, Fire Raid, Gravity Raid, Idyll Romp, Judgment, Omnislash, Ragnarok, Reflect Raid, Shock Impact, Sliding Dash, Sonic Blade, Stop Raid, Strike Raid, Stun Impact, Thunder Raid, Trinity Limit, Zantetsuken

STATS		DESCRIPTION
Strike	D+	This is the basic Keyblade attack card that you can find throughout the worlds in the game. It is fairly weak, but its availability and cheap CP requirements will keep it in your deck for a long time to come.
Thrust	D+	
Combo Finish	D+	
Swing Speed	B	
Element	PHYSICAL	
Break Recovery	B	
Required CP	☆	

CRABCLAW

LOCATION	Atlantica, random Treasure Spots.
COMBOS	Ars Arcanum, Blitz, Blizzard Raid, Firaga Break, Fire Raid, Gravity Raid, Idyll Romp, Judgment, Omnislash, Ragnarok, Reflect Raid, Shock Impact, Sliding Dash, Sonic Blade, Stop Raid, Strike Raid, Stun Impact, Thunder Raid, Trinity Limit, Zantetsuken

STATS		DESCRIPTION
Strike	C	An Atlantica-exclusive Keyblade with amazing card break recovery. This is a good, well-rounded, mid-range attack card.
Thrust	C	
Combo Finish	B+	
Swing Speed	B	
Element	PHYSICAL	
Break Recovery	☆	
Required CP	B	

PUMPKINHEAD

LOCATION	Halloween Town, random Treasure Spots.
COMBOS	Ars Arcanum, Blitz, Blizzard Raid, Firaga Break, Fire Raid, Gravity Raid, Idyll Romp, Judgment, Omnislash, Ragnarok, Reflect Raid, Shock Impact, Sliding Dash, Sonic Blade, Stop Raid, Strike Raid, Stun Impact, Thunder Raid, Trinity Limit, Zantetsuken

STATS		DESCRIPTION
Strike	C+	A Halloween Town-exclusive Keyblade that is very easy to handle and offers a fast recovery from card breaks.
Thrust	C+	
Combo Finish	D+	
Swing Speed	B	
Element	PHYSICAL	
Break Recovery	A	
Required CP	A	

SPELLBINDER

LOCATION	Hundred Acre Wood, present from Owl.
COMBOS	Ars Arcanum, Blitz, Blizzard Raid, Firaga Break, Fire Raid, Gravity Raid, Idyll Romp, Judgment, Omnislash, Ragnarok, Reflect Raid, Shock Impact, Sliding Dash, Sonic Blade, Stop Raid, Strike Raid, Stun Impact, Thunder Raid, Trinity Limit, Zantetsuken

STATS		DESCRIPTION
Strike	D+	A special attack card that is imbued with the power of Thunder. It has excellent thrust and card break recovery abilities.
Thrust	A	
Combo Finish	D+	
Swing Speed	C	
Element	LIGHTNING	
Break Recovery	A	
Required CP	B	

FAIRY HARP

LOCATION	Never Land, random Treasure Spots.
COMBOS	Ars Arcanum, Blitz, Blizzard Raid, Firaga Break, Fire Raid, Gravity Raid, Idyll Romp, Judgment, Omnislash, Ragnarok, Reflect Raid, Shock Impact, Sliding Dash, Sonic Blade, Stop Raid, Strike Raid, Stun Impact, Thunder Raid, Trinity Limit, Zantetsuken

STATS		DESCRIPTION
Strike	C+	A Never Land-exclusive Keyblade with amazing swing speed. This is another well-rounded Keyblade in the mid-range category.
Thrust	C+	
Combo Finish	C	
Swing Speed	☆	
Element	PHYSICAL	
Break Recovery	B	
Required CP	B	

METAL CHOCOBO

LOCATION	Olympus Coliseum, Key to Rewards room.
COMBOS	Ars Arcanum, Blitz, Blizzard Raid, Firaga Break, Fire Raid, Gravity Raid, Idyll Romp, Judgment, Omnislash, Ragnarok, Reflect Raid, Shock Impact, Sliding Dash, Sonic Blade, Stop Raid, Strike Raid, Stun Impact, Thunder Raid, Trinity Limit, Zantetsuken

STATS		DESCRIPTION
Strike	C+	This is a special attack card that offers well-rounded performance for a mid-range Keyblade.
Thrust	C+	
Combo Finish	B+	
Swing Speed	C	
Element	NEUTRAL	
Break Recovery	B	
Required CP	B	

WISHING STAR

LOCATION	Monstro, random Treasure Spots.
COMBOS	Ars Arcanum, Blitz, Blizzard Raid, Firaga Break, Fire Raid, Gravity Raid, Idyll Romp, Judgment, Omnislash, Ragnarok, Reflect Raid, Shock Impact, Sliding Dash, Sonic Blade, Stop Raid, Strike Raid, Stun Impact, Thunder Raid, Trinity Limit, Zantetsuken

STATS		DESCRIPTION
Strike	C	A Monstro-exclusive Keyblade that is easy to handle and has great CP requirements so you can stock more in your card deck.
Thrust	C	
Combo Finish	D+	
Swing Speed	A	
Element	PHYSICAL	
Break Recovery	A	
Required CP	A	

OLYMPIA

LOCATION	Olympus Coliseum, random Treasure Spots.
COMBOS	Ars Arcanum, Blitz, Blizzard Raid, Firaga Break, Fire Raid, Gravity Raid, Idyll Romp, Judgment, Omnislash, Ragnarok, Reflect Raid, Shock Impact, Sliding Dash, Sonic Blade, Stop Raid, Strike Raid, Stun Impact, Thunder Raid, Trinity Limit, Zantetsuken

STATS		DESCRIPTION
Strike	C+	This Olympus Coliseum-exclusive Keyblade features excellent card break recovery and CP requirements. In addition, it has better than average combo finishing abilities.
Thrust	D+	
Combo Finish	B	
Swing Speed	C	
Element	PHYSICAL	
Break Recovery	A	
Required CP	A	

WELCOME TO CASTLE OBLIVION

CHARACTERS

GAME BASICS

CASTLE OBLIVION

SECRETS OF THE GAME

THE CARDS

BESTIARY

LIONHEART

LOCATION	Traverse Town, Key to Rewards room.
COMBOS	Ars Arcanum, Blitz, Blizzard Raid, Firaga Break, Fire Raid, Gravity Raid, Idyll Romp, Judgment, Omnislash, Ragnarok, Reflect Raid, Shock Impact, Sliding Dash, Sonic Blade, Stop Raid, Strike Raid, Stun Impact, Thunder Raid, Trinity Limit, Zantetsuken

STATS		DESCRIPTION
Strike	B	This is a special Keyblade that is imbued with the power of Fire. It features better than average strength and excellent card break recovery.
Thrust	B	
Combo Finish	B	
Swing Speed	D	
Element	FIRE	
Break Recovery	A	
Required CP	B	

OATHKEEPER

LOCATION	Destiny Islands, after defeating Darkside.
COMBOS	Ars Arcanum, Blitz, Blizzard Raid, Firaga Break, Fire Raid, Gravity Raid, Idyll Romp, Judgment, Omnislash, Ragnarok, Reflect Raid, Shock Impact, Sliding Dash, Sonic Blade, Stop Raid, Strike Raid, Stun Impact, Thunder Raid, Trinity Limit, Zantetsuken

STATS		DESCRIPTION
Strike	B	This is a well-balanced Keyblade with a powerful thrust and good strength. After obtaining the first card, you can find more in Moogle Shops and Treasure Spots in Destiny Islands.
Thrust	☆	
Combo Finish	B+	
Swing Speed	B	
Element	PHYSICAL	
Break Recovery	B	
Required CP	C	

LADY LUCK

LOCATION	Wonderland, random Treasure Spots.
COMBOS	Ars Arcanum, Blitz, Blizzard Raid, Firaga Break, Fire Raid, Gravity Raid, Idyll Romp, Judgment, Omnislash, Ragnarok, Reflect Raid, Shock Impact, Sliding Dash, Sonic Blade, Stop Raid, Strike Raid, Stun Impact, Thunder Raid, Trinity Limit, Zantetsuken

STATS		DESCRIPTION
Strike	C+	A Wonderland-exclusive Keyblade that is a well-balanced, mid-range weapon with excellent speed and reasonable CP requirements.
Thrust	C+	
Combo Finish	D	
Swing Speed	A	
Element	PHYSICAL	
Break Recovery	B	
Required CP	A	

OBLIVION

LOCATION	Hallway between twelfth and thirteenth floor, after defeating Larxene.
COMBOS	Ars Arcanum, Blitz, Blizzard Raid, Firaga Break, Fire Raid, Gravity Raid, Idyll Romp, Judgment, Omnislash, Ragnarok, Reflect Raid, Shock Impact, Sliding Dash, Sonic Blade, Stop Raid, Strike Raid, Stun Impact, Thunder Raid, Trinity Limit, Zantetsuken

STATS		DESCRIPTION
Strike	A	A high-powered attack card with good strength and recovery abilities. After finding the first card, you can get more from Moogle Shops and Treasure Spots on Destiny Islands.
Thrust	A	
Combo Finish	D	
Swing Speed	C	
Element	NEUTRAL	
Break Recovery	A	
Required CP	C	

DIVINE ROSE

LOCATION	Hollow Bastion, random Treasure Spots.
COMBOS	Ars Arcanum, Blitz, Blizzard Raid, Firaga Break, Fire Raid, Gravity Raid, Idyll Romp, Judgment, Omnislash, Ragnarok, Reflect Raid, Shock Impact, Sliding Dash, Sonic Blade, Stop Raid, Strike Raid, Stun Impact, Thunder Raid, Trinity Limit, Zantetsuken

STATS		DESCRIPTION
Strike	A	This Hollow Bastion-exclusive Keyblade features a strong strike and quick swing.
Thrust	D+	
Combo Finish	C	
Swing Speed	A	
Element	PHYSICAL	
Break Recovery	C	
Required CP	B	

DIAMOND DUST

LOCATION	Castle Oblivion, treasure chest inside a Calm Bounty room, after defeating Marluxia.
COMBOS	Ars Arcanum, Blitz, Blizzard Raid, Firaga Break, Fire Raid, Gravity Raid, Idyll Romp, Judgment, Omnislash, Ragnarok, Reflect Raid, Shock Impact, Sliding Dash, Sonic Blade, Stop Raid, Strike Raid, Stun Impact, Thunder Raid, Trinity Limit, Zantetsuken

STATS		DESCRIPTION
Strike	B+	This is one of two attack cards that appear after you defeat Marluxia at the end of Sora's game. This Keyblade is strengthened by the power of the Ice element and is the fastest and easiest Keyblade to handle. After finding the first card, you can get more from Moogle Shops and Treasure Spots in Castle Oblivion.
Thrust	B+	
Combo Finish	B	
Swing Speed	☆	
Element	ICE	
Break Recovery	☆	
Required CP	C	

ONE-WINGED ANGEL

LOCATION	Twilight Town, treasure chest inside a Calm Bounty room, after defeating Marluxia.
COMBOS	Ars Arcanum, Blitz, Blizzard Raid, Firaga Break, Fire Raid, Gravity Raid, Idyll Romp, Judgment, Omnislash, Ragnarok, Reflect Raid, Shock Impact, Sliding Dash, Sonic Blade, Stop Raid, Strike Raid, Stun Impact, Thunder Raid, Trinity Limit, Zantetsuken

STATS		DESCRIPTION
Strike	C	This is one of two cards that appear after you defeat Marluxia at the end of Sora's game. It is enhanced with the Fire element and has the ability to perform excellent combo finishes. After finding the first card, you can get more from Moogle Shops and Treasure Spots in Twilight Town.
Thrust	C	
Combo Finish	☆	
Swing Speed	A	
Element	FIRE	
Break Recovery	C	
Required CP	C	

ULTIMA WEAPON

LOCATION	Castle Oblivion, inside a treasure chest from a Calm Bounty room after you've cleared both Sora and Riku modes.
COMBOS	Ars Arcanum, Blitz, Blizzard Raid, Firaga Break, Fire Raid, Gravity Raid, Idyll Romp, Judgment, Omnislash, Ragnarok, Reflect Raid, Shock Impact, Sliding Dash, Sonic Blade, Stop Raid, Strike Raid, Stun Impact, Thunder Raid, Trinity Limit, Zantetsuken

STATS		DESCRIPTION
Strike	☆	The last Keyblade found in the game! This is the strongest attack card you can find. Use it to blow away your friends in Link battles. This card can be found in all worlds after you find the first one.
Thrust	☆	
Combo Finish	A	
Swing Speed	B	
Element	PHYSICAL	
Break Recovery	B	
Required CP	D	

MAGIC CARDS

Magic cards are used to cast different spells, some element-based, some not. The magic card category is actually split into two parts when referenced in the game. There are the magic cards that include the seven cards listed in this section and the summon cards that include the seven cards in the next section. If you read the instructions for a sleight that includes a random "magic" card, this is the pool from which to choose.

FIRE

LOCATION	Hallway between first and second floors, after defeating Axel.
COMBOS	Aqua Splash, Bind, Blazing Donald, Fira, Firaga, Firaga Break, Fire Raid, Gifted Miracle, Homing Blizzara, Homing Fira, Mega Flare, Quake, Teleport
DESCRIPTION	Fire is the most basic of Fire spells. Casting it sends a fireball in the direction of the targeted enemy. To increase the power of the spell and its range of effect, stock two or three cards in combination.

BLIZZARD

LOCATION	Default card
COMBOS	Aqua Splash, Bind, Blazing Donald, Blizzara, Blizzaga, Blizzard Raid, Gifted Miracle, Homing Blizzara, Homing Fira, Quake, Teleport
DESCRIPTION	Blizzard is the most basic of the Ice spells. Casting it causes a small ice block to materialize a short distance in front of Sora, hopefully inflicting damage on an enemy. To increase the power of the spell and its range of effect, stock two or three cards in combination.

THUNDER

LOCATION	Hallway between the sixth and seventh floor, after defeating Larxene.
COMBOS	Bind, Blazing Donald, Gifted Miracle, Homing Blizzara, Homing Fira, Quake, Teleport, Thunder Raid
DESCRIPTION	Thunder is the most basic Lightning attack. Casting it causes a simple bolt of lightning to strike the targeted enemy. To increase the power and its range of effect, stock two or three cards in combination.

CURE

LOCATION	Default card
COMBOS	Bind, Blazing Donald, Cura, Curaga, Gifted Miracle, Homing Blizzara, Homing Fira, Quake, Synchro, Teleport
DESCRIPTION	Cure is the basic healing spell in the game. To increase the amount of HP recovered, stock two or three cards in combination.

GRAVITY

LOCATION	Agrabah, inside a treasure chest in the first Calm Bounty room opened.
COMBOS	Bind, Blazing Donald, Gifted Miracle, Gravira, Graviga, Gravity Raid, Homing Blizzara, Homing Fira, Quake, Synchro, Teleport, Tornado, Warpinator
DESCRIPTION	Gravity causes damage equal to 20% of the targeted enemy's HP. Stocking two and three cards in combination inflicts damage equal to 40% and 70% of the enemy's HP respectively.

STOP

LOCATION	Wonderland, inside a treasure chest in the first Calm Bounty room opened.
COMBOS	Bind, Blazing Donald, Gifted Miracle, Homing Blizzara, Homing Fira, Quake, Teleport, Warp, Warpinator
DESCRIPTION	The basic Stop spell halts the enemy's movements for two seconds. You can increase the duration of the attack to 3.5 and 6 seconds by stocking two or three cards respectively in combination. Stop does not work on all enemies and rarely on bosses.

AERO

LOCATION	Hallway between the seventh and eighth floors, after defeating Riku.
COMBOS	Aerora, Aeroga, Bind, Blazing Donald, Omnislash, Gifted Miracle, Homing Blizzara, Homing Fira, Judgment, Quake, Stop Raid, Stopra, Stopga, Synchro, Teleport, Tornado, Warp, Warpinator
DESCRIPTION	Casting Aero causes a whirlwind of air that blows enemies away from Sora while inflicting damage. To increase the effect of the spell, stock two or three cards together in a combination.

WELCOME TO CASTLE OBLIVION

CHARACTERS

GAME BASICS

CASTLE OBLIVION

SECRETS OF THE GAME

THE CARDS

BESTIARY

While these cards are grouped with magic cards, they are often referred to as summon cards within the game. Summon cards are similar to friend cards except that you actually get a physical card that you can collect and place in your deck if you choose. Unlike friend cards, this enables you to use summon cards on any floor and as part of a set attack strategy.

SIMBA

LOCATION	Traverse Town, after meeting/fighting Leon.
COMBOS	Confuse, Gifted Miracle, Proud Roar, Quake, Shock Impact, Terror, Tornado
DESCRIPTION	When called into battle, Simba replaces Sora on the field, letting out a fierce roar that inflicts damage on any Heartless standing in front of it. Stock two or three cards to add a stun effect to the roar.

DUMBO

LOCATION	Monstro, after completing the Heartless challenge in the Key to Truth room.
COMBOS	Confuse, Gifted Miracle, Splash, Terror, Tornado
DESCRIPTION	When summoned, Dumbo replaces Sora in battle and floods the enemy with water from his trunk, causing Ice element damage. Stock two or three cards to increase the amount of time this attack lasts and the area it affects.

BAMBI

LOCATION	100 Acre Wood, a gift from Pooh at end of an event.
COMBOS	Confuse, Gifted Miracle, Idyll Romp, Paradise, Terror, Tornado
DESCRIPTION	When summoned, Bambi hops around the battlefield dropping five small HP prizes. Stocking two cards makes Bambi drop five large HP prizes, while three cards adds a stun effect to the attack.

MUSHU

LOCATION	Key to Rewards room in Hollow Bastion.
COMBOS	Confuse, Firaga Break, Flare Breath, Gifted Miracle, Mega Flare, Terror, Tornado
DESCRIPTION	Mushu appears when summoned and breathes fire at the enemy, causing Fire element damage. Stock more cards to increase the duration of the attack.

GENIE

LOCATION	Agrabah, after defeating Jafar.
COMBOS	Confuse, Gifted Miracle, Showtime, Terror, Tornado
DESCRIPTION	Genie appears when called to battle and casts two spells from the following list: Stop, Gravity, and Thunder. Stocking cards in a combo increases the power of the spell cast accordingly.

TINKER BELL

LOCATION	Never Land, after defeating Captain Hook.
COMBOS	Confuse, Gifted Miracle, Terror, Tornado, Twinkle
DESCRIPTION	Tinker bell swoops down onto the battlefield and heals 30% of Sora's HP for a set period of time. Stock more cards to increase the duration and amount of healing (two cards = 60% and three cards = 100%).

CLOUD

LOCATION	Olympus Coliseum, after defeating Hades.
COMBOS	Confuse, Cross-slash, Omnislash, Gifted Miracle, Omnislash, Reflect Raid, Terror, Tornado
DESCRIPTION	This summons Cloud to the battlefield where he unleashes two devastating sword attacks. Strengthen this attack by stocking two cards to release the stronger Cross-slash attack or three cards for Omnislash. Cloud attacks the enemy (or enemies) directly in front of Sora.

Item cards are kind of different. They don't act like Potions and Elixirs do as in other RPGs, healing Sora's various afflictions in battle. Item cards in *Kingdom Hearts: Chain of Memories* are used as a substitute for reloading attack cards, magic cards, or both. In fact, the better the item card, the greater the power it has at resurrecting cards lost to card breaks, sleights or the con side of the Premium Bonus and healing your deck back to its former glory. Of course, the down side of item cards is that they are "one-time-use" only cards.

POTION

LOCATION	Default
COMBOS	Gifted Miracle, Holy, Teleport, Terror
DESCRIPTION	When used in battle, this reloads all attack cards that would be reloading during your normal recharging period. This excludes any used premium cards, card broken cards, and cards used at the beginning of a sleight.

HI-POTION

LOCATION	Olympus Coliseum, after defeating Cloud.
COMBOS	Gifted Miracle, Holy, Teleport, Terror
DESCRIPTION	This works like the Potion card, except that it reloads cards that can't be reloaded. This is a good card to have in your deck when you go up against bosses.

MEGA-POTION

LOCATION	Hallway between eleventh and twelfth floor, after defeating Riku.
COMBOS	Gifted Miracle, Holy, Teleport, Terror
DESCRIPTION	This card does the same thing as the Hi-Potion card with the added benefit of resetting the reload counter. Use this in the longer boss battles, once you've built the reload counter up to 3.

ETHER

LOCATION	Agrabah, after rescuing Jasmine from the Heartless in the Key of Guidance room.
COMBOS	Gifted Miracle, Holy, Teleport, Terror
DESCRIPTION	This card does for magic cards what Potions do for attack cards. It reloads all magic cards that would normally be reloaded during a normal recharge.

MEGA-ETHER

LOCATION	Hallway between tenth and eleventh floor, after defeating Vexen.
COMBOS	Gifted Miracle, Holy, Teleport, Terror
DESCRIPTION	This adds to the power of the Ether card by reloading those magic cards deemed "un-reloadable" in the previous rounds of play.

ELIXIR

LOCATION	Hundred Acre Wood, presented by Roo when reunited with Pooh.
COMBOS	Gifted Miracle, Holy, Teleport, Terror
DESCRIPTION	This card combines the power of Potion and Ether, immediately reloading all attack and magic cards, even those marked as un-reloadable.

MEGALIXIR

LOCATION	Destiny Islands, Key to Rewards room.
COMBOS	Gifted Miracle, Holy, Teleport, Terror
DESCRIPTION	This boosts the power of the Elixir card by resetting the reload counter in addition to reloading all magic and attack cards in Sora's deck. It is the most powerful item card in the game.

FRIEND CARDS

Friend cards only appear in battle and must be used before the battle ends. Donald and Goofy are your default friends and they appear in battle on every floor but the twelfth. As you travel through the castle, recreating worlds Sora visited in the original *Kingdom Hearts*, you will encounter other friends who will aid you during your time in that particular world. However, you cannot depend on having that friend in your "party" the entire time you are in his or her world. Some friends only join after you witness events in specific story rooms, while others join at the start of the world, but leave halfway through to take care of their own business. Once you've cleared a world and left the floor, should you return later on, your friend there will join you for the entire length of your visit. Keep in mind that there are only five worlds with friends: Agrabah, Halloween Town, Atlantica, Never Land, and Hollow Bastion.

DONALD DUCK

LOCATION	Default
COMBOS	Magic, Blazing Donald, Trinity Limit
DESCRIPTION	When you summon Donald, he randomly casts two spells from the following: Cure, Fire, Blizzard, and/or Thunder. To increase the power of these spells, stock two or more in a combo to create the Magic sleight.

GOOFY

LOCATION	Default
COMBOS	Goofy Charge, Goofy Tornado, Trinity Limit
DESCRIPTION	When called into the fray, Goofy appears in front of Sora and races across the field, smashing the enemy with his shield. Positioning is everything when you summon Goofy, since his position on the battlefield ultimately depends on yours.

ALADDIN

LOCATION	Agrabah
COMBOS	Sandstorm
DESCRIPTION	Aladdin appears on the battlefield ready to rumble! To guide his sword, run around the battlefield to the enemy rich locations. Stocking Aladdin cards into the sleight Sandstorm lengthens the effect of this summon. Aladdin is the only friend you control in this manner.

JACK

LOCATION	Halloween Town
COMBOS	Terror, Surprise! Gifted Miracle
DESCRIPTION	When called into battle, Jack casts two spells from the following list: Fire, Blizzard, Thunder, and/or Gravity. To power up his attack stock two or three cards to raise the levels of the spells cast accordingly.

ARIEL

LOCATION	Atlantica
COMBOS	Spiral Wave
DESCRIPTION	Ariel's attack is the swimming version of Goofy's. When summoned into battle, Ariel appears and swims across the battlefield, ramming into any enemy in her path. The number of cards you stock in a combo determines the number of laps she takes.

PETER PAN

LOCATION	Never Land
COMBOS	Hummingbird, Teleport
DESCRIPTION	Peter Pan's attack is similar to Ariel and Goofy's. When summoned, Peter Pan flies across the field, attacking enemies in his path with his dagger. The number of passes he makes depends on the number of Peter Pan cards you stocked into the Hummingbird sleight.

THE BEAST

LOCATION	Hollow Bastion
COMBOS	Ferocious Lunge
DESCRIPTION	Summon the Beast into battle and he lunges across the battlefield, mowing down any enemy in Sora's path. Be careful where Sora is standing so as not to waste his attack.

WELCOME TO CASTLE OBLIVION

CHARACTERS

GAME BASICS

CASTLE OBLIVION

SECRETS OF THE GAME

THE CARDS

BESTIARY

There are four types of map cards: red, green, blue, and gold. Each type has a different effect on the room created with that card. Red cards affect the Heartless in the room, creating rooms with varying number of Heartless, with Heartless of varying strength or aggressiveness, or with specific Heartless. Green cards affect battle conditions. Some increase the power of specific card classes while other cards provide an advantage in battle if you start the fight. Blue cards open up special rooms with treasure chests, save points, Moogle Shops, and so on. Finally, gold cards open special rooms like the story rooms and the hidden Rewards room. You can only carry one of these cards at a time and the Keycards to the story rooms are handed out at specific times and are not given away in battle like the others.

So the question remains: What kind of rooms do these cards open exactly? The following section contains information about each type of map card as well as a sample image of a room opened with that card. Each room has its pros and cons, but ultimately which rooms you create depend largely upon which map cards are in your inventory and your own personal taste.

RED MAP CARDS

You get access to almost half of the cards in this category at the start of the game. The other half appear once you reach the halfway point in your climb to the top of the castle. These cards determine the number, type, and strength of the Heartless in the room.

TEEMING DARKNESS

SIZE OF ROOM	Small		Medium			Large
# OF HEARTLESS	1 2 3 4 5 6 7 **8**					
QUANTITY OF TREASURE SPOTS		N/A	Few to None	Few		
		Few to Average	Average	Medium	**Many**	
DESCRIPTION	If you are looking for the larger Treasure Spots in a certain world, you can't go wrong by opening a Teeming Darkness room. This room is very large in comparison to the standard Tranquil Darkness room. As a result, it can hold more Treasure Spots and Heartless. This is a great room to create when you need to level up or collect more Moogle Points to spend in the Moogle Shops. Also, this kind of room increases the chance that an enemy will drop an enemy card at the end of a battle by 2.5x.					

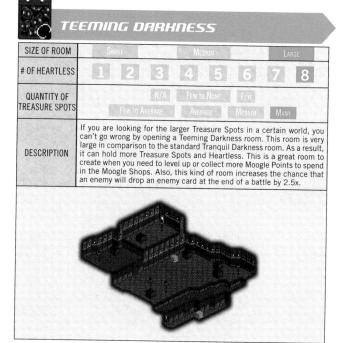

TRANQUIL DARKNESS

SIZE OF ROOM	Small		Medium			Large
# OF HEARTLESS	1 2 3 4 **5** 6 7 8					
QUANTITY OF TREASURE SPOTS		N/A	Few to None	Few		
		Few to Average	**Average**	Medium	Many	
DESCRIPTION	This is the basic room. When you enter a new floor, this is what they start you out with. Tranquil Darkness creates the most average-sized room with a moderate amount of Treasure Spots and Heartless. However, these cards start to become more rare the further you go in the Castle. If you are looking to restock your inventory, head back to the first floor and Traverse Town for the best chance to get more.					

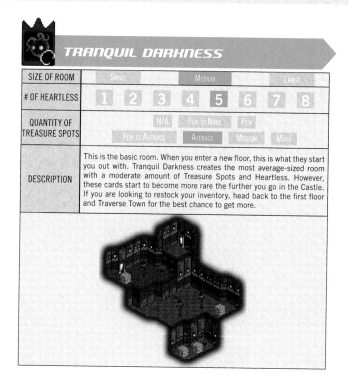

FEEBLE DARKNESS

SIZE OF ROOM	Small		Medium			Large
# OF HEARTLESS	1 2 3 4 **5** 6 7 8					
QUANTITY OF TREASURE SPOTS		N/A	Few to None	Few		
		Few to Average	Average	Medium	Many	
DESCRIPTION	The key thing about these rooms is that the Heartless have 2 points deducted from all of their cards. This makes the Feeble Darkness room the place to go to level up a little bit when the enemies in a world are a little too hard to handle.					

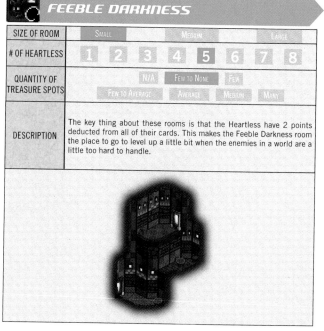

ALMIGHTY DARKNESS

SIZE OF ROOM	SMALL		MEDIUM			LARGE		
# OF HEARTLESS	1	2	3	4	5	6	7	8
QUANTITY OF TREASURE SPOTS			N/A	FEW TO NONE	FEW			
	FEW TO AVERAGE		AVERAGE		MEDIUM		MANY	
DESCRIPTION	The Almighty Darkness card creates a room that is the direct opposite of the Feeble Darkness room. This time, the enemy gets 2 points added to all of its cards, making strong monsters even stronger and weak monsters slightly more challenging. The large number of Heartless spawned in this room also makes it a good place to go for leveling up. In addition, there is an increased chance (2.5x) that enemies will drop their enemy card at the end of a successful battle.							

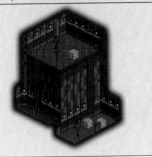

LOOMING DARKNESS

SIZE OF ROOM	SMALL		MEDIUM			LARGE		
# OF HEARTLESS	1	2	3	4	5	6	7	8
QUANTITY OF TREASURE SPOTS			N/A	FEW TO NONE	FEW			
	FEW TO AVERAGE		AVERAGE		MEDIUM		MANY	
DESCRIPTION	This room is very similar to the Teeming Darkness room. The main difference is in the aggressiveness of the Heartless. Here the Heartless are very persistent in their pursuit of trespassers. When you open a room with this card, be prepared to fight! As in the Almighty and Teeming Darkness rooms, there is an increased chance (2.5x) that the last enemy defeated in battle will drop its enemy card.							

SLEEPING DARKNESS

SIZE OF ROOM	SMALL		MEDIUM			LARGE		
# OF HEARTLESS	1	2	3	4	5	6	7	8
QUANTITY OF TREASURE SPOTS			N/A	FEW TO NONE	FEW			
	FEW TO AVERAGE		AVERAGE		MEDIUM		MANY	
DESCRIPTION	The name of the card aptly describes what you'll find inside: Sleeping Heartless. The small size of the room presents a challenge, as the Heartless inside are usually placed close to entrances and exits. Don't touch them or you'll find yourself entrenched in battle.							

PREMIUM ROOM

SIZE OF ROOM	SMALL		MEDIUM			LARGE		
# OF HEARTLESS	1	2	3	4	5	6	7	8
QUANTITY OF TREASURE SPOTS			N/A	FEW TO NONE	FEW			
	FEW TO AVERAGE		AVERAGE		MEDIUM		MANY	
DESCRIPTION	If you want to increase the chance of getting a premium prize in battle, open a room with a Premium Room card. You are granted a premium prize after defeating all of the Heartless in battle.							

WHITE ROOM

SIZE OF ROOM	SMALL		MEDIUM			LARGE	
# OF HEARTLESS	1	**2**	3	4	5	6	7	8
							(White Mushrooms only)
QUANTITY OF TREASURE SPOTS		N/A	FEW TO NONE	FEW			
	FEW TO AVERAGE		AVERAGE	MEDIUM	MANY		
DESCRIPTION	You will only encounter White Mushrooms in this overly large room. White Mushrooms are an unusual enemy in that they don't actually attack. Instead, they coax you to play a game with them. They mime what sort of spell they want to see and if you cast the right one three times in a row, you'll get a prize. Shivering indicates the need for a Fire spell; fanning indicates the need for a Blizzard spell; and drooping calls for the boost of a Thunder spell. If you get one spell wrong, the White Mushroom disappears in a huff, leaving you nothing at all. In "battles" with more than one White Mushroom, play with one at a time and isolate them from the rest so that your spells don't accidentally hit one of the others. The first time you win the game, you get a premium prize along with HP prizes and experience. When you finish playing with all of the White Mushroom on the battlefield, you get a map card (usually Calm Bounty) or perhaps the rare White Mushroom card.							

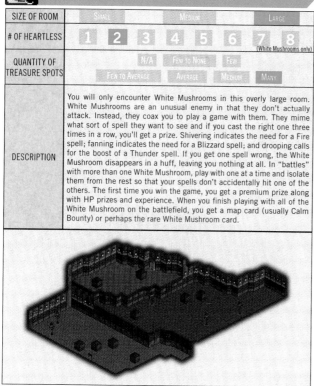

BLACK ROOM

SIZE OF ROOM	SMALL		MEDIUM			LARGE	
# OF HEARTLESS	1	**2**	3	4	5	6	7	8
							(Black Fungus only)
QUANTITY OF TREASURE SPOTS		N/A	FEW TO NONE	FEW			
	FEW TO AVERAGE		AVERAGE	MEDIUM	MANY		
DESCRIPTION	Black Funguses are the only Heartless that inhabit this room. Unlike the White Mushroom, the Black Fungus are a more warlike group. In battle, these tricksters emit clouds of spores that stun anyone caught in the way. Black Fungus are also capable of transforming into invulnerable gray mushrooms. In this form, nothing can damage them, forcing you to wait until they change back. Defeating a gang of Black Funguses nets you the standard experience prizes and a Calm Bounty card (or perhaps the rare Black Fungus card).							

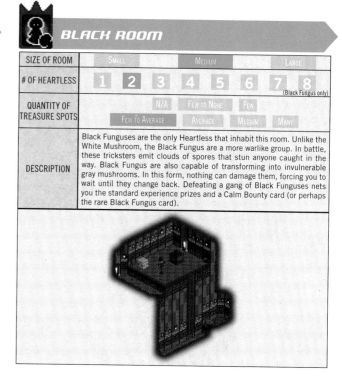

GREEN MAP CARDS

Green cards control different aspects of the battles that take place in a room. Whether you want stronger cards, weaker or slower enemies, or just an extra friend card at the start of a fight, these are the cards that will do it. You get access to the majority of the green cards after you enter the second floor of Castle Oblivion.

MARTIAL WAKING

SIZE OF ROOM	SMALL		MEDIUM			LARGE	
# OF HEARTLESS	1	2	3	4	5	**6**	7	8
QUANTITY OF TREASURE SPOTS		N/A	FEW TO NONE	FEW			
	FEW TO AVERAGE		AVERAGE	MEDIUM	MANY		
DESCRIPTION	The Waking trio of map cards gives your deck a little boost when you enter into battle in that room. Martial Waking boosts all of your attack cards by 2 points. This is great in the early part of the game when you are building your deck and high-numbered cards are tough to get. However, this +2 bonus also affects your zero cards, turning them from fabulous into somewhat weak 2 cards. For this reason, you should stop using Martial Waking cards once your deck is filled with high-numbered cards above 7 or 8.							

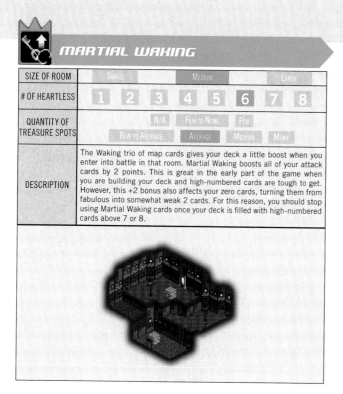

SORCEROUS WAKING

SIZE OF ROOM	SMALL		MEDIUM			LARGE	
# OF HEARTLESS	1	2	3	4	5	**6**	7	8
QUANTITY OF TREASURE SPOTS		N/A	FEW TO NONE	FEW			
	FEW TO AVERAGE		AVERAGE	MEDIUM	MANY		
DESCRIPTION	Sorcerous Waking boosts all of the magic cards in your deck by 2 points when you fight battles in that room. This card has a little more staying power than the Martial Waking card because of the difficulty in getting high-numbered magic cards and the inadvisability of using zero cards in your deck.							

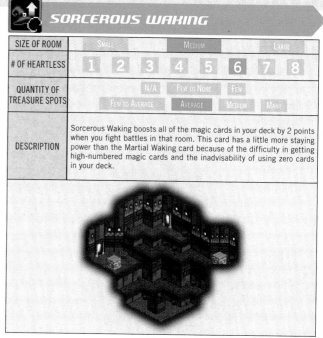

ALCHEMIC WAKING

SIZE OF ROOM	SMALL	MEDIUM	LARGE
# OF HEARTLESS	1 2 3 4	5 6	7 8
QUANTITY OF TREASURE SPOTS	N/A FEW TO NONE FEW	FEW TO AVERAGE AVERAGE	MEDIUM MANY

DESCRIPTION: Item cards receive a +2 bonus when you take on Heartless in an Alchemic Waking room. How useful this card is depends largely upon the composition of your deck. If you only use one or two item cards in your deck(s), then you only need to get one or two number 9 cards, negating the need for this card. However, until that time, this is a great way to boost your item cards' power.

STAGNANT SPACE

SIZE OF ROOM	SMALL	MEDIUM	LARGE
# OF HEARTLESS	1 2 3 4	5 6	7 8
QUANTITY OF TREASURE SPOTS	N/A FEW TO NONE FEW	FEW TO AVERAGE AVERAGE	MEDIUM MANY

DESCRIPTION: The Stagnant Space card creates a unique room that is better described as a long hallway. In here, Heartless move at half their usual speed, allowing you to dodge them more easily. Of course, the narrowness of the floor tends to work against dodging.

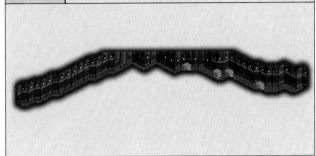

MEETING GROUND

SIZE OF ROOM	SMALL	MEDIUM	LARGE
# OF HEARTLESS	1 2 3	4 5 6	7 8
QUANTITY OF TREASURE SPOTS	N/A FEW TO NONE FEW	FEW TO AVERAGE AVERAGE	MEDIUM MANY

DESCRIPTION: This room is very similar to the Waking rooms except that instead of boosting your cards, you are given a friend card at the start of a battle. Mind you, this only works if you are in a world where your friends are available. For example, if you were to use this on the twelfth floor in Destiny Islands, nothing would happen because Goofy and Donald do not accompany you there. This card is great when you are using sleights that utilize friend cards, like the awesome Trinity Limit attack.

STRONG INITIATIVE

SIZE OF ROOM	SMALL	MEDIUM	LARGE
# OF HEARTLESS	1 2 3 4	5 6	7 8
QUANTITY OF TREASURE SPOTS	N/A FEW TO NONE FEW	FEW TO AVERAGE AVERAGE MEDIUM	MANY

DESCRIPTION: When you initiate a battle in a Strong Initiative room, you can inflict more damage with your Keyblade than normal. In new worlds where the monsters are still unfamiliar, this room provides just enough of an advantage to make a difficult battle more survivable. If you fail to start the battle, it proceeds normally with the enemy starting at full health.

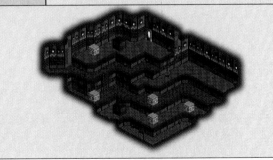

LASTING DAZE

SIZE OF ROOM	SMALL	MEDIUM	LARGE
# OF HEARTLESS	1 2 3 4	5 6	7 8
QUANTITY OF TREASURE SPOTS	N/A FEW TO NONE FEW	FEW TO AVERAGE AVERAGE	MEDIUM MANY

DESCRIPTION: When you start a battle in a Lasting Daze room, every wave of Heartless enters the battle in a stunned state, instead of just the first. If you fail to initiate the battle, the fight proceeds as normal.

WELCOME TO CASTLE OBLIVION

CHARACTERS

GAME BASICS

CASTLE OBLIVION

SECRETS OF THE GAME

THE CARDS

BESTIARY

BLUE MAP CARDS

The last main group of map cards deals almost specifically with providing special facilities on a floor. Blue cards open up rooms with Moogle Shops, save points, and treasure chests.

CALM BOUNTY

SIZE OF ROOM	Small	Medium	Large
# OF HEARTLESS	1 2	NONE	6 7 8
QUANTITY OF TREASURE SPOTS	N/A	Few to None	**Few**
	Few to Average	Average	Medium Many

DESCRIPTION: The Calm Bounty card opens a room with a single treasure chest. The first time you open up a Calm Bounty room in a world, you'll find a new card or a new sleight in the chest. In some worlds, you'll even find a new card or sleight in the second Calm Bounty room you open. The rest of the time you'll find random cards inside the chest.

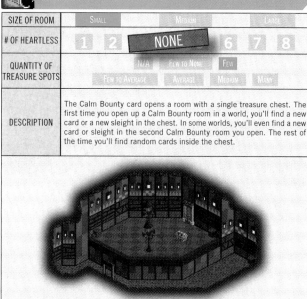

FALSE BOUNTY

SIZE OF ROOM	Small	Medium	Large
# OF HEARTLESS	1 2 3 4 5 6 **7** 8		
	(including the two inside the false treasure chests)		
QUANTITY OF TREASURE SPOTS	N/A	Few to None	**Few**
	Few to Average	Average	Medium Many

DESCRIPTION: The False Bounty card opens up a treasure room filled with three chests. Of the three, only one of the chests actually holds a prize; the rest hold Heartless. In addition to the Heartless inside the chest, other Heartless patrol the room to dissuade visitors. Of course, the contents of the true treasure chest follow the same rules as the Calm Bounty chests.

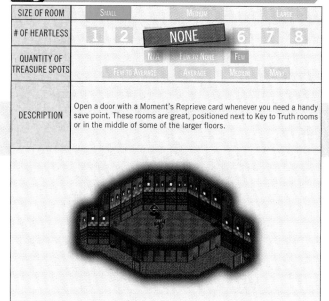

GUARDED TROVE

SIZE OF ROOM	Small	Medium	Large
# OF HEARTLESS	1 2 3 4 **5** 6 7 8		
QUANTITY OF TREASURE SPOTS	N/A	Few to None	**Few**
	Few to Average	Average	Medium Many

DESCRIPTION: If you took a Calm Bounty room and added a couple of large guards to it, you'd end up with something resembling a Guarded Trove room. Two big guards patrol the treasure along with a few normal Heartless. The contents of the treasure chest follow the same rules as the Calm Bounty chests.

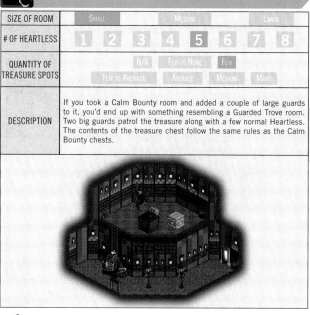

MOMENT'S REPRIEVE

SIZE OF ROOM	Small	Medium	Large
# OF HEARTLESS	1 2	NONE	6 7 8
QUANTITY OF TREASURE SPOTS	N/A	Few to None	**Few**
	Few to Average	Average	Medium Many

DESCRIPTION: Open a door with a Moment's Reprieve card whenever you need a handy save point. These rooms are great, positioned next to Key to Truth rooms or in the middle of some of the larger floors.

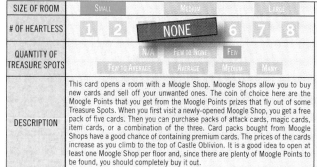

MOOGLE ROOM

SIZE OF ROOM	Small	Medium	Large
# OF HEARTLESS	1 2	NONE	6 7 8
QUANTITY OF TREASURE SPOTS	N/A	Few to None	**Few**
	Few to Average	Average	Medium Many

DESCRIPTION: This card opens a room with a Moogle Shop. Moogle Shops allow you to buy new cards and sell off your unwanted ones. The coin of choice here are the Moogle Points that you get from the Moogle Points prizes that fly out of some Treasure Spots. When you first visit a newly-opened Moogle Shop, you get a free pack of five cards. Then you can purchase packs of attack cards, magic cards, item cards, or a combination of the three. Card packs bought from Moogle Shops have a good chance of containing premium cards. The prices of the cards increase as you climb to the top of Castle Oblivion. It is a good idea to open at least one Moogle Shop per floor and, since there are plenty of Moogle Points to be found, you should completely buy it out.

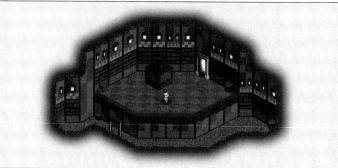

GOLD CARDS

The gold card category doesn't quite fit with the previously mentioned cards. Of the four gold cards, only one is acquired randomly at the end of battles. The rest are given as you complete the events in the story rooms in each world. The first gold card that you get in every world is the Key of Beginnings, given at the end of the opening cut-scene in the entrance room. This key is used to open the first story room. The Key of Guidance is handed out at the end of the cut-scene in the first story room and is used to open the second story room. Finally, the Key to Truth is given at the end of the events in the second story room and is used, naturally, to open the final story room.

The fourth gold card, the Key to Rewards, starts appearing at the end of battles from the seventh floor on. You can only have one of these cards in your inventory at a time, so don't hoard them! Use them to open the hidden rooms that appear on the first through the twelfth floor. Inside you'll find real treasure in the form of rare cards and powerful new sleights.

KEY OF BEGINNINGS

SIZE OF ROOM	Small		N/A		Large
# OF HEARTLESS	1	2	N/A	6	7	8
QUANTITY OF TREASURE SPOTS		N/A			
	Few to Average				Many
DESCRIPTION	This key opens up the first story room on each floor.				

KEY TO TRUTH

SIZE OF ROOM	Small		N/A		Large
# OF HEARTLESS	1	2	3	N/A	7	8
QUANTITY OF TREASURE SPOTS		N/A			
	Few to Average	N/A			Many
DESCRIPTION	This key opens up the third story room on each floor.				

KEY OF GUIDANCE

SIZE OF ROOM	Small		N/A		Large
# OF HEARTLESS	1	2	3	N/A	7	8
QUANTITY OF TREASURE SPOTS		N/A		Few	
	Few to Average	N/A		Many	
DESCRIPTION	This key opens up the second story room on each floor.				

KEY TO REWARDS

SIZE OF ROOM	Small		N/A		Large
# OF HEARTLESS	1	2	3	N/A	7	8
QUANTITY OF TREASURE SPOTS		N/A			
	Few to Average	N/A		Many	
DESCRIPTION	The Key to Rewards opens up the hidden rooms on the first through the twelfth floor. Inside you'll find the rarest treasures in the game. Key to Rewards cards start appearing on the seventh floor.				

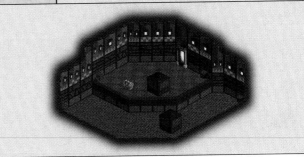

WELCOME TO CASTLE OBLIVION

CHARACTERS

GAME BASICS

CASTLE OBLIVION

SECRETS OF THE GAME

THE CARDS

BESTIARY

CARD AND SLEIGHT CHECKLIST

To aid you in your quest to collect all of the cards and sleights, we've provided a handy checklist.

THE CARDS

The following lists contain all of the cards you can physically get in the game. Absent from this list are the friend cards, since they only appear in battle.

ATTACK CARDS

- [x] Kingdom Key
- [x] Wishing Star
- [x] Lady Luck
- [x] One-Winged Angel
- [x] Three Wishes
- [x] Spellbinder
- [x] Divine Rose
- [x] Ultima Weapon
- [x] Crabclaw
- [x] Metal Chocobo
- [x] Oathkeeper
- [x] Pumpkinhead
- [x] Olympia
- [x] Oblivion
- [x] Fairy Harp
- [x] Lionheart
- [x] Diamond Dust

MAGIC AND SUMMON CARDS

- [x] Fire
- [x] Gravity
- [x] Dumbo
- [x] Tinker Bell
- [x] Blizzard
- [x] Stop
- [x] Bambi
- [x] Cloud
- [x] Thunder
- [x] Aero
- [x] Mushu
- [x] Cure
- [x] Simba
- [x] Genie

ITEM CARDS

- [x] Potion
- [x] Mega-Potion
- [x] Mega-Ether
- [x] Megalixir
- [x] Hi-Potion
- [x] Ether
- [x] Elixir

ENEMY CARDS

- [x] Shadow
- [x] Green Requiem
- [x] Barrel Spider
- [x] Gargoyle
- [x] Soldier
- [ ] Powerwild
- [ ] Search Ghost
- [ ] Pirate
- [ ] Large Body
- [ ] Bouncywild
- [ ] Sea Neon
- [ ] Air Pirate
- [ ] Red Nocturne
- [ ] Air Soldier
- [x] Screwdriver
- [x] Darkball
- [x] Blue Rhapsody
- [ ] Bandit
- [ ] Aquatank
- [ ] Defender
- [ ] Yellow Opera
- [ ] Fat Bandit
- [ ] Wight Knight
- [ ] Wyvern

- ☐ Wizard
- ☑ Neoshadow
- ☐ White Mushroom
- ☐ Black Fungus
- ☐ Creeper Plant
- ☐ Tornado Step
- ☑ Crescendo
- ☑ Guard Armor
- ☑ Parasite Cage
- ☑ Trickmaster
- ☑ Darkside
- ☑ Card Soldier
- ☑ Hades
- ☑ Jafar
- ☑ Oogie Boogie
- ☑ Ursula
- ☑ Hook
- ☑ Dragon Maleficent
- ☑ Riku
- ☑ Axel
- ☑ Larxene
- ☑ Vexen
- ☑ Marluxia
- ☑ Lexaeus
- ☑ Ansem

THE SLEIGHTS

This list contains all of the sleights learned in the course of the game.

- ☑ Aerora
- ☑ Aqua Splash
- ☑ Ars Arcanum
- ☑ Bind
- ☐ Blazing Donald
- ☑ Blitz
- ☑ Blizzaga
- ☑ Blizzara
- ☑ Blizzard Raid
- ☑ Confuse
- ☑ Cross-slash
- ☑ Cura
- ☑ Curaga
- ☑ Ferocious Lunge
- ☑ Fira
- ☑ Firaga
- ☑ Firaga Break
- ☑ Fire Raid
- ☑ Flare Breath
- ☑ Gifted Miracle

- ☑ Goofy Charge
- ☑ Goofy Tornado
- ☑ Graviga
- ☑ Gravira
- ☑ Gravity Raid
- ☑ Holy
- ☑ Homing Blizzara
- ☑ Homing Fira
- ☑ Hummingbird
- ☑ Idyll Romp
- ☑ Judgment
- ☑ Magic
- ☑ Mega Flare
- ☑ Omnislash
- ☑ Paradise
- ☑ Proud Roar
- ☑ Quake
- ☑ Ragnarok
- ☑ Reflect Raid
- ☑ Sandstorm

- ☑ Shock Impact
- ☑ Showtime
- ☑ Sliding Dash
- ☑ Sonic Blade
- ☑ Spiral Wave
- ☑ Splash
- ☐ Stop Raid
- ☑ Stopga
- ☑ Stopra
- ☑ Strike Raid
- ☐ Stun Impact
- ☑ Surprise!
- ☑ Synchro
- ☑ Teleport
- ☑ Terror
- ☑ Thundaga
- ☑ Thundara
- ☑ Thunder Raid
- ☑ Tornado
- ☑ Trinity Limit

- ☑ Twinkle
- ☑ Warp
- ☑ Warpinator
- ☑ Zantetsuken

WELCOME TO CASTLE OBLIVION

CHARACTERS

GAME BASICS

CASTLE OBLIVION

SECRETS OF THE GAME

THE CARDS

BESTIARY

THE HEARTLESS

If you played the original *Kingdom Hearts*, you will recognize almost all of the Heartless and bosses. The following entries provide each enemy's location in the game, a basic description, and information about the enemy card each enemy drops. This list is divided into two sections covering the basic Heartless you fight in each World and the special bosses.

POWERWILD

ATTACKS	Sliding, Scratch			STRONG/WEAK/ABSORB/INVULN	PHYS. ATK.	NON-ELEM	FIRE	BLIZZARD	THUNDER

Hyperactive monkey shadows that attack with th[eir hands] and feet.

ENEMY CARD POWER

Retrograde
Reverses the values of all cards. [...] 9, 2 becomes 8, etc. Cards with v[...] not affected. Lasts for one reload.

	STRONG	WEAK	ABSORB	INVULN.	PHYS. ATK.	NON-ELEM	FIRE	BLIZZARD	THUNDER
STRONG					✓	✓	✓	✓	✓
WEAK					✓	✓	✓	✓	✓
ABSORB					✓	✓	✓	✓	✓
INVULN.					✓	✓	✓	✓	✓

STATS

	1F	2F	3F	4F	5F	6F	7F	8F	9F	10F	11F	12F	13F
HP	70	77	84	91	98	105	112	119	126	133	210	224	238
AP	3	4	5	7	8	9	10	11	13	14	1	3	14
EXP	5	13	20	28	35	43	50	58	65	73	13	43	155

WORLDS FOUND

HEARTLESS QUICK-REFERENCE INFORMATION

A. WORLDS FOUND:
THE WORLDS IN WHICH THE SPECIFIC HEARTLESS CAN BE FOUND.

B. ATTACKS:
THE TYPES OF ATTACKS THE HEARTLESS USES. THIS FIELD IS NOT INCLUDED UNDER THE BOSSES SECTION. LOOK FOR THEIR CARD DECKS AND SPECIAL ATTACKS IN THE WALKTHROUGH.

C. STRENGTHS/WEAKNESSES:
EXPLAINS WHAT TYPE OF ATTACKS OR MAGIC THE HEARTLESS IS WEAK OR STRONG AGAINST. IF A HEARTLESS IS STRONG AGAINST AN ATTACK, IT MEANS THAT IT TAKES ONLY HALF THE DAMAGE AS USUAL. IF IT IS WEAK AGAINST AN ATTACK, IT TAKES 50% MORE DAMAGE THAN USUAL.

D. DESCRIPTION:
BRIEF DESCRIPTION OF THE HEARTLESS.

E. ENEMY CARD:
A BRIEF EXPLANATION OF THE POWERS GRANTED BY THE ENEMY CARD DROPPED BY THE HEARTLESS.

F. STATS:
THE BASIC STATS FOR EACH HEARTLESS IN THE SORA VERSION OF THE GAME (THE MAIN PART OF THE GAME). STATS ARE GIVEN FOR ALL FLOORS REGARDLESS OF WHETHER OR NOT THE HEARTLESS APPEARS THERE. STATS FOR THE BOSSES ARE LIMITED TO THE FLOORS ON WHICH THEY APPEAR.

AIR PIRATE

ATTACKS	Uppercut, charged punch

A winged Heartless, similar to the Air Soldier, that appears exclusively in Never Land. They attack with their fists from the air.

ENEMY CARD POWER

Item Bracer
Stop enemies from breaking item cards you use. Lasts for three reloads.

	STRONG	WEAK	ABSORB	INVULN.	PHYS. ATK.	NON-ELEM	FIRE	BLIZZARD	THUNDER
					NONE				

STATS

	1F	2F	3F	4F	5F	6F	7F	8F	9F	10F	11F	12F	13F
HP	60	66	72	78	84	90	96	102	108	114	180	192	204
AP	4	6	7	9	10	12	14	15	17	18	16	17	18
EXP	8	20	32	44	56	68	80	92	104	116	208	228	248

WORLDS FOUND

AIR SOLDIER

ATTACKS	Kick attack, thrust

These flying soldiers hover over the battlefield, swooping down to attack opponents.

ENEMY CARD POWER

Reload Kinesis
Reload while in motion. Lasts for three reloads.

	STRONG	WEAK	ABSORB	INVULN.	PHYS. ATK.	NON-ELEM	FIRE	BLIZZARD	THUNDER
					NONE				

STATS

	1F	2F	3F	4F	5F	6F	7F	8F	9F	10F	11F	12F	13F
HP	80	88	96	104	112	120	128	136	144	152	240	256	272
AP	3	4	5	7	8	9	10	11	13	14	12	13	14
EXP	5	13	20	28	35	43	50	58	65	73	130	143	155

WORLDS FOUND

AQUATANK

ATTACKS: Screw attack, thundara

Underwater Heartless who are a cross between a whale and an angler fish. These monsters attack with bursts of lightning.

ENEMY CARD POWER — Auto-Reload: Automatically reload cards when they run out. Lasts for one reload.

	PHYS. ATK.	NON-ELEM	FIRE	BLIZZARD	THUNDER
STRONG					
WEAK					
ABSORB					✓
INVULN.					

STATS

	1F	2F	3F	4F	5F	6F	7F	8F	9F	10F	11F	12F	13F
HP	130	143	156	169	182	195	208	221	234	247	390	416	442
AP	5	7	9	11	13	15	17	19	21	23	20	22	23
EXP	10	25	40	55	70	85	100	115	130	145	260	285	310

WORLDS FOUND

BANDIT

ATTACKS: Slash, rolling tackle

These foes are unique to the world of Agrabah. They are similar to the standard Soldier.

ENEMY CARD POWER — Combo Finish: Make any normal attack as strong as a finishing blow. Lasts for one reload.

	PHYS. ATK.	NON-ELEM	FIRE	BLIZZARD	THUNDER
STRONG					
WEAK			NONE		
ABSORB					
INVULN.					

STATS

	1F	2F	3F	4F	5F	6F	7F	8F	9F	10F	11F	12F	13F
HP	80	88	96	104	112	120	128	136	144	152	240	256	272
AP	5	7	9	11	13	15	17	19	21	23	20	22	23
EXP	5	13	20	28	35	43	50	58	65	73	130	143	155

WORLDS FOUND

BARREL SPIDER

ATTACKS: Explosion, body blow

Fierce spiders that look eerily like normal barrels. When you strike one, it comes to life and attacks.

ENEMY CARD POWER — Quickload: Reload cards instantly. Lasts for three reloads.

	PHYS. ATK.	NON-ELEM	FIRE	BLIZZARD	THUNDER
STRONG					
WEAK			NONE		
ABSORB					
INVULN.					

STATS

	1F	2F	3F	4F	5F	6F	7F	8F	9F	10F	11F	12F	13F
HP	60	66	72	78	84	90	96	102	108	114	180	192	204
AP	5	7	9	11	13	15	17	19	21	23	20	22	23
EXP	5	13	20	28	35	43	50	58	65	73	130	143	155

WORLDS FOUND

BLACK FUNGUS

ATTACKS: Dark poison, poison touch

Opposite of the White Mushrooms, these creatures love a good fight. Rewards are yours if you manage to defeat them.

ENEMY CARD POWER — Random Flush: Activate a random enemy card effect. Lasts for one reload.

	PHYS. ATK.	NON-ELEM	FIRE	BLIZZARD	THUNDER
STRONG					
WEAK			NONE		
ABSORB					
INVULN.					

STATS

	1F	2F	3F	4F	5F	6F	7F	8F	9F	10F	11F	12F	13F
HP	74	81	89	96	104	111	118	126	133	141	222	237	252
AP	5	7	9	11	13	15	17	19	21	23	20	22	23
EXP	1	3	4	6	7	9	10	12	13	15	26	29	31

WORLDS FOUND — BLACK ROOM ONLY

BLUE RHAPSODY

ATTACKS: Blizzard, blizzara

Small floating shadows dressed in blue cloaks that specialize in ice-based magic.

ENEMY CARD POWER — Blizzard Boost: Increases the strength of Blizzard abilities. Lasts for one reload.

	PHYS. ATK.	NON-ELEM	FIRE	BLIZZARD	THUNDER
STRONG					✓
WEAK			✓		
ABSORB				✓	
INVULN.					

STATS

	1F	2F	3F	4F	5F	6F	7F	8F	9F	10F	11F	12F	13F
HP	35	39	42	46	49	53	56	60	63	67	105	112	119
AP	3	4	5	7	8	9	10	11	13	14	12	13	14
EXP	3	8	12	17	21	26	30	35	39	44	78	86	93

WORLDS FOUND

BOUNCYWILD

ATTACKS: Slingshot, banana

The female version of the Powerwild. These clever monkeys toss banana peels in the paths of their opponents, in hopes that they'll slip and fall.

ENEMY CARD POWER — Draw: Attract fallen cards and items for easy retrieval. Lasts for five reloads.

	PHYS. ATK.	NON-ELEM	FIRE	BLIZZARD	THUNDER
STRONG					
WEAK			NONE		
ABSORB					
INVULN.					

STATS

	1F	2F	3F	4F	5F	6F	7F	8F	9F	10F	11F	12F	13F
HP	50	55	60	65	70	75	80	85	90	95	150	160	170
AP	4	6	7	9	10	12	14	15	17	18	16	17	18
EXP	5	13	20	28	35	43	50	58	65	73	130	143	155

WORLDS FOUND

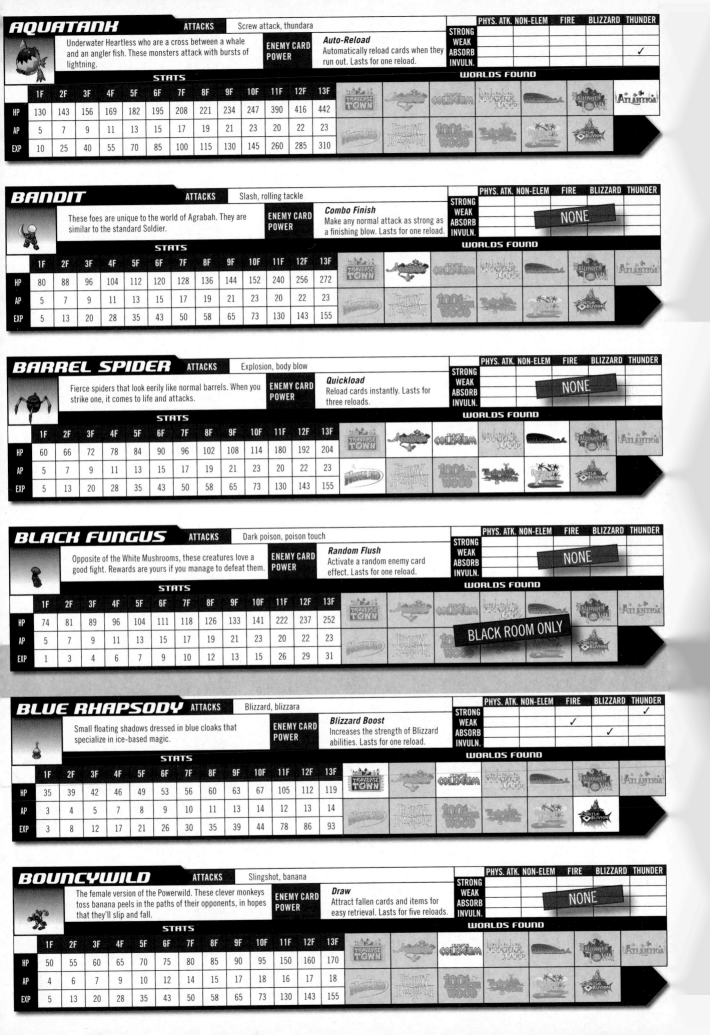

CREEPER PLANT

ATTACKS: Seed attack, root needle

A type of Heartless that looks like a flower. These creatures attack using their roots and seeds.

ENEMY CARD POWER

Leaf Bracer
Stop enemies from breaking Cure abilities you use. Lasts for one reload.

	PHYS. ATK.	NON-ELEM	FIRE	BLIZZARD	THUNDER
STRONG					
WEAK	NONE				
ABSORB					
INVUL.					

STATS

	1F	2F	3F	4F	5F	6F	7F	8F	9F	10F	11F	12F	13F
HP	60	66	72	78	84	90	96	102	108	114	180	192	204
AP	3	4	5	7	8	9	10	11	13	14	12	13	14
EXP	8	20	32	44	56	68	80	92	104	116	208	228	248

WORLDS FOUND

CRESCENDO

ATTACKS: Trumpet attack, trumpet healing

A strange Heartless that resembles a cross between a bird and a horn. These creatures can honk and call to other Heartless.

ENEMY CARD POWER

Summon Boost
Forfeit magic card use to power up summon cards. Lasts for one reload.

	PHYS. ATK.	NON-ELEM	FIRE	BLIZZARD	THUNDER
STRONG					
WEAK	NONE				
ABSORB					
INVUL.					

STATS

	1F	2F	3F	4F	5F	6F	7F	8F	9F	10F	11F	12F	13F
HP	70	77	84	91	98	105	112	119	126	133	210	224	238
AP	3	4	5	7	8	9	10	11	13	14	12	13	14
EXP	8	20	32	44	56	68	80	92	104	116	208	228	248

WORLDS FOUND

DARKBALL

ATTACKS: Bite, float

Large floating balls made up of darkness. They weave around the battlefield, suddenly attacking their opponents.

ENEMY CARD POWER

Cardblind
Hide the cards you hold from hostile eyes. Lasts for three reloads.

	PHYS. ATK.	NON-ELEM	FIRE	BLIZZARD	THUNDER
STRONG					
WEAK	NONE				
ABSORB					
INVUL.					

STATS

	1F	2F	3F	4F	5F	6F	7F	8F	9F	10F	11F	12F	13F
HP	70	77	84	91	98	105	112	119	126	133	210	224	238
AP	3	4	5	7	8	9	10	11	13	14	12	13	14
EXP	10	25	40	55	70	85	100	115	130	145	260	285	310

WORLDS FOUND

DEFENDER

ATTACKS: Fira, shield bite

A heavily armored version of the Large Body Heartless. These monsters attack with their shields and shoot fireballs at enemies.

ENEMY CARD POWER

Protect
Decrease damage from physical attacks by the enemy. Magical attacks cause normal damage. Lasts for one reload.

	PHYS. ATK.	NON-ELEM	FIRE	BLIZZARD	THUNDER
STRONG					
WEAK				✓	✓
ABSORB					
INVUL.	✓				

STATS

	1F	2F	3F	4F	5F	6F	7F	8F	9F	10F	11F	12F	13F
HP	90	99	108	117	126	135	144	153	162	171	270	288	306
AP	4	6	7	9	10	12	14	15	17	18	16	17	18
EXP	13	33	52	72	91	111	130	150	169	189	338	371	403

WORLDS FOUND

FAT BANDIT

ATTACKS: Beat down, fireball

Similar to the Large Body, these bandits are unique to the world of Agrabah.

ENEMY CARD POWER

Back Attacks
Increases damage when striking enemies from behind. Lasts for two reloads.

	PHYS. ATK.	NON-ELEM	FIRE	BLIZZARD	THUNDER
STRONG					
WEAK					
ABSORB					
INVUL.	✓				

STATS

	1F	2F	3F	4F	5F	6F	7F	8F	9F	10F	11F	12F	13F
HP	120	132	144	156	168	180	192	204	216	228	360	384	408
AP	5	7	9	11	13	15	17	19	21	23	20	22	23
EXP	10	25	40	55	70	85	100	115	130	145	260	285	310

WORLDS FOUND

GARGOYLE

ATTACKS: Wing attack, fira

Living gargoyles that fly about the battlefield pelting their opponents with fireballs. These creatures can only be found in Halloween Town.

ENEMY CARD POWER

Vanish
Become invisible and reduce your chances of being hit. Lasts for one reload.

	PHYS. ATK.	NON-ELEM	FIRE	BLIZZARD	THUNDER
STRONG					
WEAK	NONE				
ABSORB					
INVUL.					

STATS

	1F	2F	3F	4F	5F	6F	7F	8F	9F	10F	11F	12F	13F
HP	80	88	96	104	112	120	128	136	144	152	240	256	272
AP	4	6	7	9	10	12	14	15	17	18	16	17	18
EXP	5	13	20	28	35	43	50	58	65	73	130	143	155

WORLDS FOUND

GREEN REQUIEM

ATTACKS: Cure

Small floating shadows dressed in green cloaks that specialize in Cure magic.

ENEMY CARD POWER

Cure Boost — Increases the strength of Cure abilities. Lasts for one reload.

	PHYS. ATK.	NON-ELEM	FIRE	BLIZZARD	THUNDER
STRONG					
WEAK					
ABSORB			✓	✓	✓
INVULN.					

STATS

	1F	2F	3F	4F	5F	6F	7F	8F	9F	10F	11F	12F	13F
HP	40	44	48	52	56	60	64	68	72	76	120	128	136
AP	2	3	4	4	5	6	7	8	8	9	8	9	9
EXP	3	8	12	17	21	26	30	35	39	44	78	86	93

WORLDS FOUND

LARGE BODY

ATTACKS: Jumping shockwave, body blow

These large, rotund soldiers can deflect attacks to their front. Their round bodies are unmistakable—and difficult to dodge past.

ENEMY CARD POWER

Guard — Deflect frontal physical attacks and completely nullify damage. Lasts for one reload.

	PHYS. ATK.	NON-ELEM	FIRE	BLIZZARD	THUNDER
STRONG					
WEAK		NONE			
ABSORB					
INVULN.					

STATS

	1F	2F	3F	4F	5F	6F	7F	8F	9F	10F	11F	12F	13F
HP	100	110	120	130	140	150	160	170	180	190	300	320	340
AP	4	6	7	9	10	12	14	15	17	18	16	17	18
EXP	10	25	40	55	70	85	100	115	130	145	260	285	310

WORLDS FOUND

NEOSHADOW

ATTACKS: Scratch, shadow out

These are souped-up versions of the standard Shadow. They are fierce opponents who can turn into two-dimensional shadows and melt into the floor.

ENEMY CARD POWER

Bio — Cause enemies' HP to gradually drop. Lasts for one reload.

	PHYS. ATK.	NON-ELEM	FIRE	BLIZZARD	THUNDER
STRONG					
WEAK		NONE			
ABSORB					
INVULN.					

STATS

	1F	2F	3F	4F	5F	6F	7F	8F	9F	10F	11F	12F	13F
HP	74	81	89	96	104	111	118	126	133	141	222	237	252
AP	3	4	5	7	8	9	10	11	13	14	12	13	14
EXP	10	25	40	55	70	85	100	115	130	145	260	285	310

WORLDS FOUND

PIRATE

ATTACKS: Slash & walk, charged slash

A more powerful version of the Soldier who dwells exclusively in Never Land. When their swords flash, they deal a blow that stuns their opponents.

ENEMY CARD POWER

All Zeros — Changes the values of all your cards to 0. Lasts for one reload.

	PHYS. ATK.	NON-ELEM	FIRE	BLIZZARD	THUNDER
STRONG					
WEAK		NONE			
ABSORB					
INVULN.					

STATS

	1F	2F	3F	4F	5F	6F	7F	8F	9F	10F	11F	12F	13F
HP	70	77	84	91	98	105	112	119	126	133	210	224	238
AP	4	6	7	9	10	12	14	15	17	18	16	17	18
EXP	8	20	32	44	56	68	80	92	104	116	208	228	248

WORLDS FOUND

POWERWILD

ATTACKS: Sliding, scratch

Hyperactive monkey shadows that attack with their fists and feet.

ENEMY CARD POWER

Retrograde — Reverses the values of all cards. 1 becomes 9, 2 becomes 8, etc. Cards with value 0 are not affected. Lasts for one reload.

	PHYS. ATK.	NON-ELEM	FIRE	BLIZZARD	THUNDER
STRONG					
WEAK		NONE			
ABSORB					
INVULN.					

STATS

	1F	2F	3F	4F	5F	6F	7F	8F	9F	10F	11F	12F	13F
HP	70	77	84	91	98	105	112	119	126	133	210	224	238
AP	3	4	5	7	8	9	10	11	13	14	12	13	14
EXP	5	13	20	28	35	43	50	58	65	73	130	143	155

WORLDS FOUND

RED NOCTURNE

ATTACKS: Fire, fira

Small floating shadows dressed in red cloaks that specialize in fire-based magic.

ENEMY CARD POWER

Fire Boost — Increases the strength of Fire abilities. Lasts for one reload.

	PHYS. ATK.	NON-ELEM	FIRE	BLIZZARD	THUNDER
STRONG					✓
WEAK				✓	
ABSORB			✓		
INVULN.					

STATS

	1F	2F	3F	4F	5F	6F	7F	8F	9F	10F	11F	12F	13F
HP	35	39	42	46	49	53	56	60	63	67	105	112	119
AP	3	4	5	7	8	9	10	11	13	14	12	13	14
EXP	3	8	12	17	21	26	30	35	39	44	78	86	93

SEA NEON

ATTACKS: Body blow, screw attack

These are underwater versions of the basic Shadow enemy.

ENEMY CARD POWER

Random Values — Randomize the values of cards you use. Lasts for one reload.

	PHYS. ATK.	NON-ELEM	FIRE	BLIZZARD	THUNDER
STRONG					
WEAK					✓
ABSORB					
INVULN.					

STATS

	1F	2F	3F	4F	5F	6F	7F	8F	9F	10F	11F	12F	13F
HP	50	55	60	65	70	75	80	85	90	95	150	160	170
AP	4	6	7	9	10	12	14	15	17	18	16	17	18
EXP	4	10	16	22	28	34	40	46	52	58	104	114	124

WORLDS FOUND

SEARCH GHOST

ATTACKS: HP absorption, slap

These ghostly shadows have the ability to warp around the battlefield. They can also drain an opponent's HP.

ENEMY CARD POWER

Drain — Absorb enemy HP when striking with attack cards, but enemies will drop fewer items. Lasts for one reload.

	PHYS. ATK.	NON-ELEM	FIRE	BLIZZARD	THUNDER
STRONG			NONE		
WEAK					
ABSORB					
INVULN.					

STATS

	1F	2F	3F	4F	5F	6F	7F	8F	9F	10F	11F	12F	13F
HP	60	66	72	78	84	90	96	102	108	114	180	192	204
AP	3	4	5	7	8	9	10	11	13	14	12	13	14
EXP	5	13	20	28	35	43	50	58	65	73	130	143	155

WORLDS FOUND

SCREWDRIVER

ATTACKS: Slash, rolling attack

Fierce underwater Heartless that attack foes with their sharp spears.

ENEMY CARD POWER

Decrementor — Decrease the values of all cards by 1. Lasts for one reload.

	PHYS. ATK.	NON-ELEM	FIRE	BLIZZARD	THUNDER
STRONG					
WEAK					
ABSORB					✓
INVULN.					

STATS

	1F	2F	3F	4F	5F	6F	7F	8F	9F	10F	11F	12F	13F
HP	80	88	96	104	112	120	128	136	144	152	240	256	272
AP	5	7	9	11	13	15	17	19	21	23	20	22	23
EXP	8	20	32	44	56	68	80	92	104	116	208	228	248

WORLDS FOUND

SHADOW

ATTACKS: Scratch, thrust

Shadows are the basic Heartless enemy. They are small creatures that have the ability to become two-dimensional when threatened.

ENEMY CARD POWER

Incrementor — Increases the value of all cards by 1 point. Lasts for two reloads.

	PHYS. ATK.	NON-ELEM	FIRE	BLIZZARD	THUNDER
STRONG			NONE		
WEAK					
ABSORB					
INVULN.					

STATS

	1F	2F	3F	4F	5F	6F	7F	8F	9F	10F	11F	12F	13F
HP	33	36	40	43	46	50	53	56	59	63	99	106	112
AP	2	3	4	4	5	6	7	8	8	9	8	9	9
EXP	3	8	12	17	21	26	30	35	39	44	78	86	93

WORLDS FOUND

SOLDIER

ATTACKS: Scratch, screw kick

This is the soldier form of the basic Shadow. They are slightly more aggressive and powerful than Shadows.

ENEMY CARD POWER

Combo Plus — Adds an extra hit to normal combos. Lasts for three reloads.

	PHYS. ATK.	NON-ELEM	FIRE	BLIZZARD	THUNDER
STRONG					
WEAK			NONE		
ABSORB					
INVULN.					

STATS

	1F	2F	3F	4F	5F	6F	7F	8F	9F	10F	11F	12F	13F
HP	60	66	72	78	84	90	96	102	108	114	180	192	204
AP	3	4	5	7	8	9	10	11	13	14	12	13	14
EXP	5	13	20	28	35	43	50	58	65	73	130	143	155

WORLDS FOUND

TORNADO STEP

ATTACKS: Charged propeller, jump attack

These creatures like to spin around the battlefield using their long arms like propeller blades.

ENEMY CARD POWER

Reload Haste — Subtract 2 from the reload counter. Lasts for one reload.

	PHYS. ATK.	NON-ELEM	FIRE	BLIZZARD	THUNDER
STRONG					
WEAK			NONE		
ABSORB					
INVULN.					

STATS

	1F	2F	3F	4F	5F	6F	7F	8F	9F	10F	11F	12F	13F
HP	70	77	84	91	98	105	112	119	126	133	210	224	238
AP	3	4	5	7	8	9	10	11	13	14	12	13	14
EXP	8	20	32	44	56	68	80	92	104	116	208	228	248

WORLDS FOUND

WHITE MUSHROOM

ATTACKS None

Strange creatures that only want to play a game with you. If you can figure out what their gestures mean, they will reward you.

ENEMY CARD POWER

Hyper Healing Restore some HP each time you use a friend card. Lasts for three reloads.

	PHYS. ATK.	NON-ELEM	FIRE	BLIZZARD	THUNDER
STRONG					
WEAK			NONE		
ABSORB					
INVULN.					

WORLDS FOUND — WHITE ROOM ONLY

STATS

	1F	2F	3F	4F	5F	6F	7F	8F	9F	10F	11F	12F	13F
HP	198	218	238	257	277	297	317	337	356	376	594	634	673
AP	0	0	0	0	0	0	0	0	0	0	0	0	0
EXP	3	8	12	17	21	26	30	35	39	44	78	86	93

WIGHT KNIGHT

ATTACKS Slash, rolling attack

These zombie-like troops, known for their extremely long limbs, are unique to Halloween Town.

ENEMY CARD POWER

Float Alter gravity to increase jumping ability. Lasts for three reloads.

	PHYS. ATK.	NON-ELEM	FIRE	BLIZZARD	THUNDER
STRONG					
WEAK			NONE		
ABSORB					
INVULN.					

STATS

	1F	2F	3F	4F	5F	6F	7F	8F	9F	10F	11F	12F	13F
HP	70	77	84	91	98	105	112	119	126	133	210	224	238
AP	4	6	7	9	10	12	14	15	17	18	16	17	18
EXP	8	20	32	44	56	68	80	92	104	116	208	228	248

WIZARD

ATTACKS Thundara, blizzara, fira

These Heartless are proficient in magic and can cast high-level Fire, Blizzard, and Thunder spells.

ENEMY CARD POWER

Magic Boost Forfeit summon cards use to power up magic cards. Lasts for one reload.

	PHYS. ATK.	NON-ELEM	FIRE	BLIZZARD	THUNDER
STRONG					
WEAK					
ABSORB				✓	✓	✓
INVULN.					

(ABSORB: FIRE ✓, BLIZZARD ✓, THUNDER ✓)

STATS

	1F	2F	3F	4F	5F	6F	7F	8F	9F	10F	11F	12F	13F
HP	50	55	60	65	70	75	80	85	90	95	150	160	170
AP	3	4	5	7	8	9	10	11	13	14	12	13	14
EXP	10	25	40	55	70	85	100	115	130	145	260	285	310

WYVERN

ATTACKS Kick, rush attack

A large, winged Heartless that attacks its foes from the sky, headbutting them across the field or slashing at their face with their talons.

ENEMY CARD POWER

Reload Lock Reload without incrementing the reload counter. Lasts for three reloads.

	PHYS. ATK.	NON-ELEM	FIRE	BLIZZARD	THUNDER
STRONG					
WEAK			NONE		
ABSORB					
INVULN.					

STATS

	1F	2F	3F	4F	5F	6F	7F	8F	9F	10F	11F	12F	13F
HP	70	77	84	91	98	105	112	119	126	133	210	224	238
AP	4	6	7	9	10	12	14	15	17	18	16	17	18
EXP	10	25	40	55	70	85	100	115	130	145	260	285	310

YELLOW OPERA

ATTACKS Rush attack, thunder

Small, floating shadows dressed in yellow cloaks. They specialize in lightning-based magic.

ENEMY CARD POWER

Thunder Boost Increases the strength of Thunder abilities. Lasts for one reload.

	PHYS. ATK.	NON-ELEM	FIRE	BLIZZARD	THUNDER
STRONG					
WEAK					
ABSORB					✓
INVULN.					

STATS

	1F	2F	3F	4F	5F	6F	7F	8F	9F	10F	11F	12F	13F
HP	35	39	42	46	49	53	56	60	63	67	105	112	119
AP	3	4	5	7	8	9	10	11	13	14	12	13	14
EXP	3	8	12	17	21	26	30	35	39	44	78	86	93

ANSEM

Sora and Riku's nemesis from the original *Kingdom Hearts*. Through Sora defeated Ansem's physical form, his shadow lives on in the depths of Riku's heart, constantly taunting him.

ENEMY CARD POWER

Sleightblind
Conceals the cards you've stocked for a sleight from your opponents. Lasts for five sleights, adds resistance to fire, ice and lightning.

	PHYS. ATK.	NON-ELEM	FIRE	BLIZZARD	THUNDER
STRONG		✓	✓	✓	✓
WEAK					
ABSORB					
INVULN.					

STATS

	B12F	B11F	B10F	B9F	B8F	B7F	B6F	B5F	B4F	B3F	B2F	B1F	13F
HP	400	-	-	-	-	-	-	-	-	-	-	2240	
AP	3	-	-	-	-	-	-	-	-	-	-	25	
EXP	133	-	-	-	-	-	-	-	-	-	-	0	

WORLDS FOUND

RIKU MODE

AXEL

A member of the mysterious Organization. This character seems to have his own agenda that may or may not agree with the Organization's. In battle, he is a fierce competitor who uses fire magic to fry his opponents.

ENEMY CARD POWER

Quick Recovery
Use cards even while staggering from damage. Lasts for 10 hits taken, adds immunity to fire but makes you stunned by ice.

	PHYS. ATK.	NON-ELEM	FIRE	BLIZZARD	THUNDER
STRONG		✓			✓
WEAK					
ABSORB			✓		
INVULN.					

STATS

	1F	2F	3F	4F	5F	6F	7F	8F	9F	10F	11F	12F	13F
HP	320	-	-	-	-	-	-	-	-	-	-	-	1680
AP	2	-	-	-	-	-	-	-	-	-	-	-	15
EXP	75	-	-	-	-	-	-	-	-	-	-	-	6825

WORLDS FOUND

CARD SOLDIER

These cards are soldiers in the Queen of Hearts' army. Their fear for her temper compels them to do anything she asks. The Card Soldiers act like normal Shadow soldiers when in battle.

ENEMY CARD POWER

Attack Haste
Increase the swing speed of attack cards. Lasts for 30 attacks.

	PHYS. ATK.	NON-ELEM	FIRE	BLIZZARD	THUNDER
STRONG					
WEAK			✓		
ABSORB					
INVULN.					

STATS

	1F	2F	3F	4F	5F	6F	7F	8F	9F	10F	11F	12F	13F
HP	-	88	96	104	112	120	-	-	-	-	-	-	-
AP	-	4	5	7	8	9	-	-	-	-	-	-	-
EXP	-	13	20	28	35	43	-	-	-	-	-	-	-

WORLDS FOUND

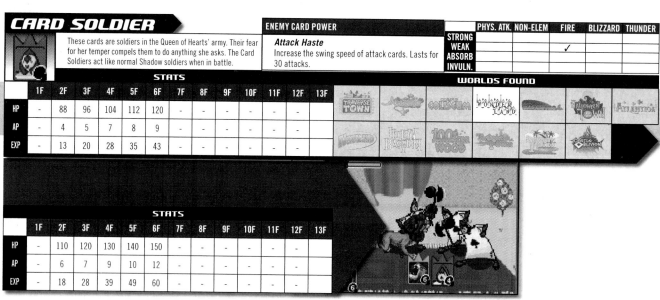

STATS

	1F	2F	3F	4F	5F	6F	7F	8F	9F	10F	11F	12F	13F
HP	-	110	120	130	140	150	-	-	-	-	-	-	-
AP	-	6	7	9	10	12	-	-	-	-	-	-	-
EXP	-	18	28	39	49	60	-	-	-	-	-	-	-

DARKSIDE

This is the Heartless that attacked Sora's home on Destiny Islands at the start of the original *Kingdom Hearts*. This boss shoots energy balls at its foes or tries to intimidate foes with its massive size and strength.

ENEMY CARD POWER

Mimic
Copy the enemy card your opponent is using. Nothing happens if your opponent has no enemy card in play.

	PHYS. ATK.	NON-ELEM	FIRE	BLIZZARD	THUNDER
STRONG		✓	✓	✓	✓
WEAK					
ABSORB					
INVULN.					

STATS

	1F	2F	3F	4F	5F	6F	7F	8F	9F	10F	11F	12F	13F
HP	-	-	-	-	-	-	-	-	-	-	-	1920	-
AP	-	-	-	-	-	-	-	-	-	-	-	26	-
EXP	-	-	-	-	-	-	-	-	-	-	-	5558	-

WORLDS FOUND

DRAGON MALEFICENT

An old foe responsible for turning Riku to the dark side. She steals Belle's pure heart to increase her powers. When Sora and his friends attempt to take the heart back, she takes the form of a powerful dragon to drive her opponents away.

ENEMY CARD POWER

Overdrive: Sacrifice reload speed to power up attack cards. Lasts for 30 attacks.

	PHYS. ATK.	NON-ELEM	FIRE	BLIZZARD	THUNDER
STRONG		✓	✓	✓	✓
WEAK					
ABSORB					
INVULN.					

STATS

	1F	2F	3F	4F	5F	6F	7F	8F	9F	10F	11F	12F	13F
HP	-	-	-	-	-	-	960	1020	1080	1140	-	-	-
AP	-	-	-	-	-	-	17	19	21	23	-	-	-
EXP	-	-	-	-	-	-	1730	1990	2249	2509	-	-	-

WORLDS FOUND

GUARD ARMOR

This Heartless haunts Traverse Town, appearing when the bells ring to wreak havoc on the town. This monster can detach his hands and feet to extend his attack range. After destroying those appendages, his limbless torso and head start spinning around the battlefield.

ENEMY CARD POWER

Wide Attacks

Slightly extends the range of attack cards. Lasts for 30 attacks.

	PHYS. ATK.	NON-ELEM	FIRE	BLIZZARD	THUNDER
STRONG		✓	✓	✓	✓
WEAK					
ABSORB					
INVULN.					

STATS

	1F	2F	3F	4F	5F	6F	7F	8F	9F	10F	11F	12F	13F
HP	200	-	-	-	-	-	-	-	-	-	-	-	-
AP	5	-	-	-	-	-	-	-	-	-	-	-	-
EXP	48	-	-	-	-	-	-	-	-	-	-	-	-

WORLDS FOUND

HADES

Ruler of the Underworld who has a serious grudge against Hercules. He's a fierce competitor who doesn't like to lose. Uses blue flame to smite his enemies.

ENEMY CARD POWER

Berserk

Boosts the power of attack cards when low on HP (when the gauge is flashing red). Lasts for 30 attacks, adds resistance to fire, but makes you stunned by ice.

	PHYS. ATK.	NON-ELEM	FIRE	BLIZZARD	THUNDER
STRONG		✓			
WEAK					
ABSORB			✓		
INVULN.					✓

STATS

	1F	2F	3F	4F	5F	6F	7F	8F	9F	10F	11F	12F	13F
HP	-	440	480	520	560	600	-	-	-	-	-	-	-
AP	-	6	7	9	10	12	-	-	-	-	-	-	-
EXP	-	233	372	512	651	791	-	-	-	-	-	-	-

WORLDS FOUND

HOOK

Captain Hook is a pirate who holds a grudge against Peter Pan. To get back at his young foe, he kidnaps his friend Wendy in the hopes that Peter Pan will come and rescue her. How will he react when he learns that Peter Pan comes with backup?

ENEMY CARD POWER

Second Chance

Retain 1HP after a critical hit, provided you have 2 or more HP left. Lasts for three uses, adds resistance to lightning, but makes you stunned by fire.

	PHYS. ATK.	NON-ELEM	FIRE	BLIZZARD	THUNDER
STRONG		✓		✓	
WEAK					
ABSORB					
INVULN.					✓

STATS

	1F	2F	3F	4F	5F	6F	7F	8F	9F	10F	11F	12F	13F
HP	-	-	-	-	-	-	640	680	720	760	-	-	-
AP	-	-	-	-	-	-	10	11	13	14	-	-	-
EXP	-	-	-	-	-	-	1730	1990	2249	2509	-	-	-

WORLDS FOUND

JAFAR

This sorcerer has an overwhelming desire to become the ruler of Agrabah using any means necessary. When he steals the magic lamp from Aladdin, he uses one of his wishes to become super powerful.

ENEMY CARD POWER

Attack Bracer

Stop enemies from breaking attack cards you use. Lasts for 20 attacks.

	PHYS. ATK.	NON-ELEM	FIRE	BLIZZARD	THUNDER
STRONG		✓	✓	✓	✓
WEAK					
ABSORB					
INVULN.					

STATS

	1F	2F	3F	4F	5F	6F	7F	8F	9F	10F	11F	12F	13F
HP	-	550	600	650	700	750	-	-	-	-	-	-	-
AP	-	7	9	11	13	15	-	-	-	-	-	-	-
EXP	-	233	372	512	651	791	-	-	-	-	-	-	-

WORLDS FOUND

LARXENE

A member of the mysterious Organization. Larxene is the most vengeful of the group and distrusts and dislikes everyone. In battle, she is a swift opponent who uses lightning attacks to stun and wound her foes.

ENEMY CARD POWER

Dash
Increases running speed. Lasts for 15 cards, adds immunity to lightning but makes you weak against special attacks.

	PHYS. ATK.	NON-ELEM	FIRE	BLIZZARD	THUNDER
STRONG			✓	✓	
WEAK					
ABSORB					
INVULN.					

STATS

	1F	2F	3F	4F	5F	6F	7F	8F	9F	10F	11F	12F	13F
HP	-	-	-	-	-	1120	-	-	-	-	-	-	-
AP	-	-	-	-	-	5	-	-	-	-	-	15	-
EXP	-	-	-	-	-	2325	-	-	-	-	-	6263	-

WORLDS FOUND

HALLWAYS BETWEEN FLOORS 6-7 AND 12-13

LEXAEUS

No. 5 in the Organization, Lexaeus attempts to conquer Riku and bend him to his will.

ENEMY CARD POWER

Warp Break
Obliterates enemies with the finishing blow of a combo with a high success rate. During versus battles, this can stun your opponent. Lasts for 50 attacks, adds immunity to ice and resistance to physical attacks, but makes you weak against special attacks.

	PHYS. ATK.	NON-ELEM	FIRE	BLIZZARD	THUNDER
STRONG	✓		✓		✓
WEAK					
ABSORB					
INVULN.				✓	

STATS

	1F	2F	3F	4F	5F	6F	7F	8F	9F	10F	11F	12F	13F
HP	-	-	-	-	-	-	-	-	1680	-	-	-	-
AP	-	-	-	-	-	-	-	-	15	-	-	-	-
EXP	-	-	-	-	-	-	-	-	6517	-	-	-	-

WORLDS FOUND

RIKU MODE

MARLUXIA

Lord of Castle Oblivion, Marluxia seeks to acquire Sora's power.

ENEMY CARD POWER

Double Sleight
Use stocked cards and sleights twice in a row. However, during versus mode battles this bumps up the reload counter. Lasts for three sleights, adds resistance to fire, ice, lightning, and special attacks but makes you weak against physical attacks.

	PHYS. ATK.	NON-ELEM	FIRE	BLIZZARD	THUNDER
STRONG	✓	✓	✓	✓	✓
WEAK	✓	✓	✓	✓	✓
ABSORB	✓	✓	✓	✓	✓
INVULN.	✓	✓	✓	✓	✓

STATS

	1F	2F	3F	4F	5F	6F	7F	8F	9F	10F	11F	12F	13F
HP	-	-	-	-	-	-	-	-	-	-	-	-	2240
AP	-	-	-	-	-	-	-	-	-	-	-	-	27
EXP	-	-	-	-	-	-	-	-	-	-	-	-	13131

WORLDS FOUND

STATS

	1F	2F	3F	4F	5F	6F	7F	8F	9F	10F	11F	12F	13F
HP	-	-	-	-	-	-	-	-	-	-	-	-	2244
AP	-	-	-	-	-	-	-	-	-	-	-	-	28
EXP	-	-	-	-	-	-	-	-	-	-	-	-	0

OOGIE BOOGIE

The mischevious villan is always plotting against poor Jack Skellington. When he steals Dr. Finklestein's potion, he gets a bit more than he expects, as the potion drives him mad with fear.

ENEMY CARD POWER

Regen
Gradually restores HP. HP return more quickly when Sora's gauge is low. Lasts for 10 uses.

	PHYS. ATK.	NON-ELEM	FIRE	BLIZZARD	THUNDER
STRONG		✓	✓		✓
WEAK	✓				
ABSORB					
INVULN.					

STATS

	1F	2F	3F	4F	5F	6F	7F	8F	9F	10F	11F	12F	13F
HP	-	550	600	650	700	750	-	-	-	-	-	-	-
AP	-	7	9	11	13	15	-	-	-	-	-	-	-
EXP	-	233	372	512	651	791	-	-	-	-	-	-	-

WORLDS FOUND

PARASITE CAGE

This Heartless dwells inside Monstro's stomach, protected by pools of acid. Sora is forced to fight it when it takes Pinocchio hostage in its belly.

ENEMY CARD POWER

Dispel
Break an opponent's enemy card without fail. Nothing occurs if your opponent has no enemy card in play.

	PHYS. ATK	NON-ELEM	FIRE	BLIZZARD	THUNDER
STRONG		✓	✓	✓	✓
WEAK					
ABSORB					
INVULN.					

STATS

	1F	2F	3F	4F	5F	6F	7F	8F	9F	10F	11F	12F	13F
HP	-	605	660	715	770	825	-	-	-	-	-	-	-
AP	-	6	7	9	10	12	-	-	-	-	-	-	-
EXP	-	233	372	512	651	791	-	-	-	-	-	-	-

WORLDS FOUND

RIKU

One of Sora's best childhood friends along with Kairi. He was seduced to the side of darkness by Maleficent and Ansem and took up arms against Sora. At the present time his whereabouts are unknown.

ENEMY CARD POWER

Sleight Lock
Keep cards used in sleights available for reloading. Lasts for five sleights, adds resistance to fire, ice and lightning.

	PHYS. ATK	NON-ELEM	FIRE	BLIZZARD	THUNDER
STRONG		✓	✓		
WEAK					
ABSORB					
INVULN.					

STATS

	1F	2F	3F	4F	5F	6F	7F	8F	9F	10F	11F	12F	13F
HP	-	-	-	-	-	-	1120	1120	-	-	1120	1680	-
AP	-	-	-	-	-	-	5		-	-	10	-	-
EXP	-	-	-	-	-	-	2775	3225	-	-	5700	6825	-

WORLDS FOUND

HALLWAYS BETWEEN FLOORS 7-8, 8-9, 11-12, 12-13

TRICKMASTER

The Trickmaster is behind the theft of the Queen of Hearts' memories. This gangly juggler uses flaming sticks to attack its foes.

ENEMY CARD POWER

Value Break
When you lose a card break, this reduces the value of the enemy's card by the value of your broken card. Lasts for 10 breaks.

	PHYS. ATK	NON-ELEM	FIRE	BLIZZARD	THUNDER
STRONG		✓	✓		
WEAK					
ABSORB					
INVULN.					

STATS

	1F	2F	3F	4F	5F	6F	7F	8F	9F	10F	11F	12F	13F
HP	-	550	600	650	700	750	-	-	-	-	-	-	-
AP	-	7	9	11	13	15	-	-	-	-	-	-	-
EXP	-	233	372	512	651	791	-	-	-	-	-	-	-

WORLDS FOUND

URSULA

Ursula thinks she found the perfect plan to seize control of Atlantica: kidnap the Princess Ariel's friend, Flounder, and make her give up her father's trident in return for her friend's safety. Unfortunately things don't go as she plans…

ENEMY CARD POWER

Shell
Halves the damage from magical attacks by the enemy. Summon magic does normal damage. Lasts for five hits taken.

	PHYS. ATK	NON-ELEM	FIRE	BLIZZARD	THUNDER
STRONG		✓	✓		
WEAK					
ABSORB					
INVULN.					

STATS

	1F	2F	3F	4F	5F	6F	7F	8F	9F	10F	11F	12F	13F
HP	-	-	-	-	-	-	640	680	720	760	-	-	-
AP	-	-	-	-	-	-	17	19	21	23	20	22	23
EXP	-	-	-	-	-	-	1730	1990	2249	2509	-	-	-

WORLDS FOUND

VEXEN

A member of the Organization in charge of research, Vexen creates the replica of Riku to test Sora's power. He uses ice magic in battle and holds a large ice shield that protects him from frontal assaults.

ENEMY CARD POWER

Auto-Life
Revive automatically when your HP reaches 0. Only a small amount of HP is restored. Lasts for a single use, adds immunity to ice, but you will be stunned by fire.

	PHYS. ATK	NON-ELEM	FIRE	BLIZZARD	THUNDER
STRONG		✓			
WEAK					
ABSORB				✓	
INVULN.		✓			

STATS

	1F	2F	3F	4F	5F	6F	7F	8F	9F	10F	11F	12F	13F
HP	-	-	-	-	-	-	-	-	-	-	1120	1120	-
AP	-	-	-	-	-	-	-	-	-	-	15	20	-
EXP	-	-	-	-	-	-	-	-	-	-	4125	5700	-

WORLDS FOUND

TO SAVE THEIR WORLD, YOU'LL HAVE TO BECOME PART OF IT.

JOIN TRON AND MERCURY IN AN EPIC BATTLE FOR THE VIRTUAL WORLD

A SINISTER COMPUTER PROGRAM HAS UNLEASHED A DEADLY VIRUS INTO THE SYSTEM. NOW, YOU MUST BECOME A DIGITAL WARRIOR, GOING DEEP INTO THIS DANGEROUS REALM TO HELP ALLIES TRON AND MERCURY DELETE THE CORRUPTOR AND HIS POWERFUL ARMY. JOURNEY THROUGH 30 HEART-POUNDING LEVELS, USING AN ARSENAL OF WEAPONS AND HI-TECH VEHICLES. IT'S ACTION SO INTENSE, YOUR GAME BOY® WILL NEVER BE THE SAME AGAIN...NEITHER WILL YOU.

ISBN: 0-7440-0473-X

Library of Congress Catalog No.: 2004114055

Printing Code: The rightmost double-digit number is the year of the book's printing; the rightmost single-digit number is the number of the book's printing. For example, 04-1 shows that the first printing of the book occurred in 2004.

07 06 05 04   4 3 2 1

Manufactured in the United States of America.

BRADYGAMES STAFF

Publisher
David Waybright

Editor-In-Chief
H. Leigh Davis

Director of Marketing
Steve Escalante

Marketing Manager
Janet Eshenour

Creative Director
Robin Lasek

Licensing Manager
Mike Degler

Assistant Marketing Manager
Susie Nieman

Team Coordinator
Stacey Beheler

CREDITS

Title Manager
Tim Cox

Screenshot Editor
Michael Owen

Book Designer
Doug Wilkins

Production Designer
Wil Cruz